THE NORTH AMERICAN ITALIAN RENAISSANCE

ITALIAN WRITING IN AMERICA AND CANADA

To Michele

Good Luck with Primo

Regards,

John Acorn bie

11-16-05

Alver. JJLaVerne

ESSAY SERIES 43

Canada

Guernica Editions Inc. acknowledges the financial support of the Government of Canada through the Book Publishing Industry Development Program (BPIDP).

Kenneth Scambray

The North American Italian Renaissance

Italian Writing in America and Canada

Guernica
Toronto·Buffalo·Lancaster (U.K.)
2000

Antonio D'Alfonso, editor.

Guernica Editions Inc.

P.O. Box 117, Station P, Toronto (ON), Canada M5S 2S6

2250 Military Road, Tonawanda, N.Y. 14150-6000 U.S.A.

Gazelle, Falcon House, Queen Square, Lancaster LA1 1RN U.K.

Typesetting by Selina.
Printed in Canada.

Legal Deposit – Third Quarter
National Library of Canada
Library of Congress Catalog Card Number: 00-101692
Canadian Cataloguing in Publication Data
Scambray, Kenneth
The North American Italian renaissance :
Italian writings in America and Canada
(Essay series ; 43)
Included bibliographical references.
ISBN 1-55071-107-5

1. American literature – Italian American authors – History and criticism.

2. Canadian literature (English) — Italian Canadian authors – History and criticism. 3. American literature – 20th century – History and criticism.

4. Canadian literature (English) – 20th century – History and criticism.

I. Title. II. Series: Essay Series (Toronto, Ont.) ; 43.

PS8089.5.I8S33   2000   810.9'851   C00-901017-3

PR9185.6.I8S33 2000

Table of Contents

ITALIAN CANADIAN WRITERS

THE ITALIAN AMERICAN AUTOBIOGRAPHY

DISCOVERY AND DEFINITION ITALIAN AMERICAN WOMEN WRITERS

POETIC VOICES:
NORTH AMERICAN ITALIAN POETRY

SICILIAN POETRY IN AMERICA

Acknowledgments

This book is the result of the selflessness and generosity of many people. I owe a special debt of gratitude to two editors of *L'Italo-Americano* Mario Trecco and Fr. Augusto Feccia. All but two of the following essays have appeared in *L'Italo-Americano* since 1987. I want to thank Mario Trecco for his faith in my proposal to him over twenty years ago. We met in the old office of the newspaper near St. Peter's Italian Church that once anchored Los Angeles' Little Italy. I proposed that in the face of a renaissance in Italian American writing *L'Italo-Americano* needed a book review column. During his tenure as editor, from 1990 to 1998, Fr. Augusto Feccia was equally encouraging in both the freedom and support he has extended to me in my writing. Over lunch and espresso at the newspaper's new office at Villa Scalabrini in Sun Valley, we spoke often about the role and significance of *L'Italo-Americano* for the Italian communities in California, Oregon, and Washington. I want to thank the editors of *Italian Americana* for permission to reprint the portions of the essays on Rachael Guido deVries and Anne Paolucci. Aris Janigian provided helpful and insightful comments for the revision of my introduction. I have benefitted greatly from Laura Stortoni's many suggestions as friend and colleague. Without Antonio D'Alfonso's encouragement and sagacious advice, this work would not have been possible. I owe a special debt of gratitude to my wife, Carole, who has read this manuscript as carefully and tirelessly as she has the thousands of student themes she has assigned over her years as an English teacher.

This book is dedicated to the memory of my father Marion Scambray (Schembri – the original form of my Sicilian name) and to my mother Josephine Di Filippo Scambray. It is to them I owe everything: my life and my heritage. The narrative I tell here began at our dinner table when I was a boy growing up in Fresno.

Ai miei genitori
che hanno ispirato
questo libro

Introduction

CHALLENGING HOMOGENEITY

Each individual is not only the synthesis of existing relations, but also the history of these relations, the sum of all of the past.

Antonio Gramsci, *Prison Notebooks*

Since the nineteenth century, ethnic literature in America has been relegated to the margins of American literary history. However, at the end of the twentieth century the ever growing production of ethnic literature, including Native American and African American writers, has questioned the definition of American cultural identity. Whose culture is it? Who should be allowed to define the centrist culture, if indeed one even exists? How can the disparate voices of ethnic identities in America ever contribute to a unified cultural fabric? If the cultural centrists' resistance to canonical change is not enough, there are internecine battles among ethnic critics. Some ethnic critics are attempting to exclude from the category of ethnic literature Jews, Italians, and other European groups. Further, some homosexual critics have attempted, as well, to exclude Jews and Italians from the homosexual community on the basis that their degree of persecution in "white" heterosexual society is not sufficient to merit inclusion in their history of discrimination against people "of color." Aside from the destructiveness of these internecine ethnic battles, the current culture war in America is by no means unique to American literary history. Actually, canonical revision and even the challenge to a centrist notion of American literature are at the very core of American literary history.

Ralph Waldo Emerson fired the first salvo in America's culture wars when he wrote at the beginning of the nineteenth century: "Our age is retrospective. It builds the sepulchres of its fathers." In *Nature* and in his many essays, he called for writing that was based solely on the American experience and free from European influences. Though he did not reject entirely the influence of European ideas in America, he felt that the European-dominated canon did not allow room for the native American voice to be heard. America's patriarchs of high culture, content to translate Dante and Virgil and teach Shakespeare at Harvard, would not listen to his eccentric voice. Cooper, Longfellow, Holmes, Whittier, Bryant, Stowe, and a host of other popular writers of the century held the center with their Europeanized poems and romances. All other literary productions, including women's writing and slave and capture narratives, remained on the margins, even though some had reached a wide, popular readership. It would take nearly two centuries before writers such as William Wells Brown, Frederick Douglass, and Harriet Jacobs would find a secure place next to the canonized writers of the nineteenth century.

By century's end, the cultural challenge that Emerson issued to his generation blossomed into a full-scale culture war in the essays of William Dean Howells. Echoing what Emerson had written a generation before, Howells ignited a culture war known as the "war over literary realism" that remains profoundly relevant to the efforts to revise the American canon today.

Beginning with his nine years as editor of the Boston *Atlantic Monthly* (1872-1881) and extending to his "Editor's Easy Chair" column in *Harper's Monthly* (1886-1892) in New York, Howells championed the cause of a new kind of American literature and advocated the complete revision of the American literary canon. He argued that European writers – from Jane Austen in England,

Björnstjerne Björnson in Norway, Giovanni Verga in Italy, Armando Valdés in Spain, to Émile Zola in France, and Ivan Turgenev in Russia – formed an international realistic movement in prose fiction. But what impressed Howells most about these writers was that they all wrote about their own native experiences. Like Emerson before him, he asked why can't American writers portray the American character and American experience in their novels. In his essays and reviews, he urged American writers to avoid the influence of the historical and sentimental romance and to represent in a realistic form their own American experiences. In retrospect, it seems axiomatic that Howells and his many supporters would win the cultural war: who should speak for American culture but American voices?

The battle that Howells waged has been termed the war over literary realism. But it can be identified just as accurately as the war over literary regionalism. From the perspective of the end of the twentieth century, Howells was advocating the development of a national literature that reflected the diversity of American culture. His was not a formalistic argument. For sure, he emphasized the realistic form, but realism was merely the vehicle needed to express the experiences of American writers wherever they found themselves. Nor was he troubled over the question, raised often by his critics, of how a unified, national identity could be fashioned out of the regional diversity that existed in the United States at the time.

In defense of American regionalism, he argued that in their own way each of the great European novelists were parochial because they addressed only the concerns of their particular class or countries and even, in the case of Verga, their regions. When Howells reviewed the sum of American literature in the 1880s and 90s – from Henry James' upper-class Americans abroad, Sarah Orne Jewett's Maine Villagers, Mary E. Wilkins' New Englanders, John W. De Forest's Southerners, and Henry Blake Fuller's Chicago businessmen, to E. W.

Howe's, Joseph Kirkland's and Hamlin Garland's rural Mid-westerners – he saw a breadth in American literature that was not diminished in the least in comparison with European fiction.

In contemporary terms, Howells brought the regionalist margins of American literature into its cultural center. From New York he argued for a decentered canon that was geographically dispersed. He successfully challenged the homogeneous, centrist notion of American culture preached from the academic pulpits of New England. His critics complained that regionalist novelists, with their parochial, low-brow characters, whether farm boys, big city businessmen, or James' provincial *nouveau riche* abroad, were not sufficiently idealized. They belabored the boring and inessential details of their provincial characters' lives. Too often the life so graphically depicted in a rural hamlet or in a Chicago business office was sordid and depressing. Such works lacked the transcendence found in Shakespeare or even Jane Austen.

Regionalism was attacked in the same terms that ethnic literature has been attacked over the last thirty years. As Allan Bloom argues in *The Closing of the American Mind*, "Men may live more truly and fully in reading Plato and Shakespeare than at any other time, because then they are participating in essential being and are forgetting their accidental lives." Similarly, Howells' regionalist writers were accused of focusing on the "accidental details" of their characters' economically and morally bankrupt lives. Howells faced torrents of protests from critics who did not want to see the new industrial reality or class warfare represented in the nation's fiction. The social Darwinism of the period became in the novel literary naturalism, in which characters' fates were indeed accidental, based on the whims of *laissez-faire* capitalism.

Ultimately, Howells and the novelists he promoted won the culture war. The European influence in American letters was sufficiently expunged to allow for the development of the novel based on the regional diversity of the American experience.

Howells' legacy extended into the 1920s where, under the influence of scholars and writers such as Vernon L. Parrington, Perry Miller, F. O. Matthiessen, and Alfred Kazin, the American canon was established for at least the next half century. However, Howells' hard-fought victory over regionalism was almost immediately overridden in the 1920s and 30s by new totalizing theories of American culture, from historical theories of economic democracy and Puritanism to formalistic aesthetics of symbolism and realism. While class would play a significant part in the criticism of Alfred Kazin's left-wing criticism, gender and ethnicity would be absent in all the hegemonic theories proposed by the pre-World War II critics and university professors.

Ironically, Humbert Nelli in *Italians in Chicago* writes that, by 1910, first- and second-generation European ethnics accounted for on the average more than 75% of the population of America's five largest northeastern cities. Regional diversity in America was now augmented by ethnic diversity. No sooner had American critics and scholars established a totalizing definition of American culture, based in large part on formalistic, symbolic aesthetics and on an Anglo-Saxon Protestant-Puritan tradition, the demographic foundation of the country had shifted radically. Over thirteen million immigrants flooded into America before the 1920s exclusion laws slowed immigration, especially from southern Europe. This was a canon that was ripe for revision before the ink was dried. Though American professors and critics chose to ignore the potential impact of the new immigrants, Antonio Gramsci understood well the influence that America's ethnic diversity, including African American writers and intellectuals, would soon have on American culture. From his prison cell in the 1930s, he wrote that American cultural equilibrium would "arise out of the need to fuse together in a single national crucible the different types of culture brought in by immigrants of diverse national origins."

As Gramsci anticipated, American culture and the culture war that has raged over the last thirty years is infinitely more complex than Howells' earlier battle over literary regionalism. His war was simplistically bi-polar: the romance versus the novel, Europe versus America. Today, the culture wars that are raging over the definitions of American and Canadian cultures, as well as elsewhere in the world, are infinitely more complex and dispersed. As Canadian critic Francesco Loriggio explains in his introduction to *Social Pluralism and Literary History*, in our post-modern period "if there are observations to be made, they are not quite the either/or kind." The critic today, in Loriggio's terms, still must deal with "the second 'post' – post colonialism – and its tangencies with the first – postmodernism – about the re-envisioning of Europe and European culture, and about questions of race, gender, and ethnicity." In "DissemiNation: time, narrative, and the margins of the modern nation," Homi K. Bhabha attempts to locate a "disjunctive" and dispersed view of "cultural difference" in society. He writes that once a nation is defined, then "the threat of cultural difference is no longer a problem of 'other' people. It becomes a question of the otherness of the people-as-one." This remark is as applicable to Howells' argument for a decentered, regional literature in the nineteenth century as it is to the battle over the canon today.

By appealing to Howells' culture war, I am assuming that literary history does retain some authority to inform us. The current culture war over multiculturalism and canonical revision finds its parallel if not resolution in Howells' successful battle over literary regionalism. American literary history provides, in Bhabha's words, not only a "narrative authority for marginal voices," but also locates the topic of diversity at the very center of the American narrative tradition. The nineteenth-century debate over literary regionalism teaches us that ethnic writing, from its origins to the post-war period, has always been a significant aspect of the diverse American experience. What is left is to define the pieces of that pluriculturalism.

North American Italian Writing

National identity, language, and cultural unity within the (post)modern state are just some of the complex aspects of the multicultural discourse that do not allow for facile answers. Furthermore, the Italic critic must address not only those who presume to speak from the so-called cultural center in North America, but even some supporters of pluriculturalism. In Canada, as Antonio D'Alfonso explains in *In Italics*, Italians must contend with the French and English camps: if writers do not write in French or English, then they do not have a voice. Similarly, American society has created "racial" categories of European Americans, African Americans, Asian Americans, Latino Americans, and Native Americans. Some have attempted to reduce these "racial" categories to a simplistic "White and of Color" model. Italian Americans have been assigned by some to the "white race." These "racial" categories now occupy the center of the discourse over multiculturalism.

In *Race Matters* Cornel West writes, "Without the presence of black people in America, European-Americans would not be "white" – they would be *only* (my Italics) Irish, Italians, Poles, Welsh, and others engaged in class, ethnic, and gender struggles over resources and identity." In the first place, the struggle to define an Italic Tradition in America, Canada, Germany, Australia, and elsewhere in the world is an effort to overcome being defined as "only" white or "only" Australian. We are attempting to define the aspects of the Italic culture that have been transplanted in other cultures throughout the world. As Gramsci wrote, "every individual is not only a synthesis of existing relations, but also the history of these relations, the sum of all of the past." In *Italian Signs, American Streets: The Evolution of Italian American Narrative*, Fred Gardaphé has written a seminal work defining at least one approach to the history of the Italic narrative in America. Ironically, at the precise historical moment when Italians in North America are attempting to define their narrative voice, we suddenly find that we have become only a "synthesis of existing relations" without a past. Similarly, poet Rose Romano explains in "Coming Out Olive in the Lesbian Community" that Italian women find themselves marginalized even in the homosexual community because they have no place in the "hierarchy of pain" that people "of color" have arbitrarily expropriated for themselves. As Sneja Gunew points out in "Multicultural Multiplicities: Canada, U.S.A. and Australia," those who appeal to unhistorical black-white racial distinctions are merely "reinstating traditional essentialist constructions of race" into the multicultural discourse.

The complex historical beginnings of Italian immigration defy easy synthesis, though stereotypes of Italian immigrants still prevail. As D'Alfonso explains, Italians did not necessarily come to North America for economic reasons: "The reasons for their departure are manifold, even though people enjoy reducing the causes to the economy of the times." D'Alfonso suggests that Italian immigrants attempted to transcend the boundaries of a homogeneous national identity that was about to be imposed on them once again in the wake of the Risorgimento. Pasquale Verdicchio suggests in "Subalterns Abroad" that the Risorgimento "did not liberate the South; it merely altered the colonial structure" of Italy. Southern Italian immigrants came as refugees from their own form of colonization.

Unlike the rest of Europe, Italy did not have a colonial past. Rather, before 1860, the Italian peninsula endured wave after wave of foreign invaders and colonizers. Indeed, the same king, Holy Roman Emperor of Spain, Charles V, that dispatched the conquistadors to the New World to massacre the Aztecs in 1521 under Cortès and annihilated the Incas under Pizarro in 1531, sacked and destroyed Rome in 1527. For over five hundred years the same Spanish Bourbon house, the French, and the Vatican, including the Pope's powerful bishops in northern city states, formed alliances and went to war over Naples to control southern Italy, Sicily included. In the eighteenth and nineteenth centuries the roads of Calabria in the south of Italy, under the rule of French or Spanish kings, were strewn with the decapitated heads and bodies of rebelling southern Italians. Such brutalization extended back to the Renaissance when Pope Sixtus V, in a crackdown on brigandage, festooned the walls of the Castle St. Angelo with the heads of the rebellious poor.

The history of this brutal colonization and exploitation is one reason why southern Italians fled to America. As Loriggio suggests, the notion of an imperial European culture "was probably more of an abstraction to them [immigrants] than the idea of America." Rome and the Church with all its wealth were viewed by Italian immigrants as their oppressors, not as proud aspects of their cultural heritage. In the "Southern Question," Antonio Gramsci articulated accurately the Italian ruling class's view of southern Italian peasants: "the South is a lead weight which impedes a more rapid civil development of Italy; southerners are biologically inferior beings, semi-barbarians or complete barbarians by natural destiny."

As Loriggio points out, to ignore history is to de-culturalize the multicultural debate in America and to racialize society. This is both bad science and bad history. The hyphenated "racial" categories are in reality ethnic categories, subjects for cross-cultural study. In the 1960s, the Irish American priest Andrew Greeley was among the first sociologists to discover ethnicity in America. Similarly, in the 1980s and 90s African American scholar Thomas Sowell has made learned cross-cultural studies of ethnicity in America that focus on cultural differences, not racial.

To de-culturalize the debate over multiculturalism in American society is to express the same tired, hegemonic notion that Israel Zangwill presented in his melodramatic play *The Melting-Pot*. De-culturalizing the multicultural debate and racializing society is a means of creating a new center, what I call the "racial centrist view," and new margins. It should matter little to Italians in North America whether we are considered assimilated into Israel Zangwill's Anglo-Saxon melting pot or lumped into the amalgamated "white race" of Euro-Americans. To place Italians in America in the "white race" denies locating a specific Italic Tradition in North America. As D'Alfonso argues, to place Italians in a similar category would be to allow the English and French their tidy and simplistic bi-polar cultural war and to deny the voice of approximately thirteen million ethnics, including a million and a half Italians, in Canada.

The essays that follow represent a cross-section of the Italian American and Italian Canadian literature written over the last thirty years. As Joseph Pivato writes in *Echo*, his study of Canadian and Australian Italian writing, the field of Italian ethnic writing did not exist much before 1978. He writes that when he began his study, "What I discovered came as a shock. These other voices were not strange, but echoes of my voice; in fact, echoes of our voices as the sons and daughters of immigrants. I discovered that the other was me." Like Pivato, what I have discovered in my reading is that this voice we hear in the North American Italian narrative is interdependent. The shock of recognition is no greater in a novel or poem than it is in a study of history, folklore, or sociology. My categories, including history, sociology, and folklore, before we get to fiction and poetry, are intended to suggest a methodology for the study of North American Italian literature. These works form a coherent part of the Italic narrative in North America that echo each other, only in different forms and voices. The North American Italian narrative cannot be viewed separately from history and culture.

In 1980, in *The Italian Americans: Troubled Roots,* Andrew Rolle asked where the Italian American novelists are, like other ethnic writers such as O.E. Rölvaag, Anzia Yezierska, William Saroyan, and Philip Roth, who have written the "Italian version of big-city life and its clash with old values"? In 1992 at a conference on immigration Gay Talese asked a similar question. For sure, Italian immigrants did not come to America with sufficient education to begin producing novels in great numbers in the

1920s and 30s. But what is more important is that contemporary historians and critics have not had the benefit of ample scholarship and criticism on the abundant North American Italian writing that has been produced since 1945. As Helen Barolini has argued in a trenchant essay entitled "The Case of the Missing Italian Writers," the issue is not so much the silence of Italian American writers in the twentieth century as the silence that has surrounded their works. Since the turn of the century, Italian American writers have represented well the inner-city experiences they faced as immigrants and the clash between the Old World and the New – from di Donato, Tomasi, and Fante to the novels of Puzo, Barolini, and Mirabelli. Ferlinghetti, di Prima, Corso, and Lamantia are writers that influenced the course of contemporary American poetry. Di Donato's *Christ in Concrete* has been out of print until only recently while Tina De Rosa's *Paper Fish,* a remarkable work about the conflict between the old and the new, remained out of print for over fifteen years after its publication in 1980. What Pivato discovered in Canadian literature in 1978 was not a paucity of Italian fiction or poetry but a critical silence, delimiting both its commercial appeal and denying its location in Canadian culture. What follows is only a small but important representation of the historical breach in that silence in what can be called *The North American Italian Renaissance* in literature.

Understanding the Past

LA STORIA IN ITALY AND NORTH AMERICA

La Storia: Five Centuries of the Italian American Experience
by Jerre Mangione and Ben Morreale

Mangione and Morreale have written an extraordinarily valuable history. It is a work that must rank as a major contribution to the history of Italians in America. At the same time, however, its point of view is also limited by the current condition of Italian studies in the United States. In one sense there is little original research in the volume. Most of the information is derived from other already published research on the Italian influence in America. But that is not a criticism of the infinitely readable presentation and style of the work. *La Storia* is not a dry recitation of facts. Rather, it reads like an epic that covers history's single greatest immigration of people from one continent to another. It documents the roots of the North American Italian narrative, from its parochial origins in Italy to its dynamic development in the 1990s. It belongs on the shelf with the first complete study of Italians in America, Robert F. Foerster's *The Italian Emigration of Our Times* (1919).

La Storia begins with an overview of the early Italian explorers of the New World and of what we know about Italians among the colonizers. But the real substance of the text begins with Chapter 3, "Italians Before and After Unification." Here Mangione/Morreale document the oppressive political conditions and the poverty that forced southern Italians to emigrate to

America. During the nearly two hundred years of Bourbon rule, the peasants of the *mezzogiorno* and Sicily were little more than chattel. Under the rule of the Kingdom of the Two Sicilies, as southern Italy and Sicily were called before unification, the peasant population was ruled by a series of foreign despots, ending with the reign of Frederick II in 1859. The peasants of the south were taxed beyond their means and lived under unspeakable conditions.

Unfortunately, the pillaging of the south by foreign despots and their armies left a legacy that would not be reversed, even after Garibaldi and the unification of Italy in 1870. As Booker T. Washington, born as an American slave, wrote upon visiting Italy at the turn of the century, "The Negro is not the man farthest down. The condition of the colored farmer in the most backward parts of the Southern States in America, even where he has the least education and least encouragement, is incomparably better than the condition and opportunities of the agricultural population in Sicily." The grinding poverty of the nineteenth century continued unabated into the twentieth century.

As Mangione/Morreale point out, little more than a decade after the unification of Italy, immigration began at an alarming rate, "reducing Italy's population by one third" before it was over. More than three million Italian immigrants arrived in America alone, the vast majority from the south. The basic impetus for this mass migration was "economic survival." However, the southern peasant's urge to emigrate went beyond economics. As a people who had been colonized by the North for centuries, the southern peasant "did not feel any strong degree of allegiance towards the new nation." As one immigrant explained, "Where I gain my crust of bread, there is my country."

As a result, America became the dream of the southern peasant. However, upon their arrival, they discovered that their battle for economic and social justice was only just beginning. *Mannaggia La Merica* would become their collective curse during their years of economic struggle. Mangione/Morreale document the battle that the immigrants faced, from their landing at Ellis Island and Louisiana, to their migration across the vast expanse of America in search of jobs and a better way of life. They document the prejudice they faced, from low wages and marginal jobs to the infamous lynching of eleven Italians by a New Orleans mob in 1891. In response to their conditions, Italians became leaders in the labor movement. Their involvement in radical politics further stigmatized them in American cities as a despised, foreign element. The hostility against Italians was expressed finally in the trial, conviction, and execution of Sacco and Vanzetti.

Mangione/Morreale speak from a distinct point of view. In telling the story of Italians' struggle to assimilate into American life, they focus upon the positive side of Italian American life. Aside from Andrew Rolle's *The Immigrant Upraised*, this side of the Italian American experience has seldom been told. As a result, Mangione/Morreale turn a critical eye upon some of our most successful artists, such as Coppola, Puzo, and Scorsese, for their depiction of the wrong image of Italians in their works. Inadvertently, Mangione/Morreale raise the complex question of what it means to assimilate into American society. In their negative appraisal of the works of Coppola, Puzo, Scorsese, Cimino, and Stallone, Mangione/Morreale seem to attribute their individual and collective failures as artists to the fact that "The further one gets from the world of the early immigrants, the less socially aware the filmmakers seem to become. . . "

This sounds too much like the older generation chastising the younger generation for growing up and away from their working-class, family values. Are Mangione/Morreale expressing the ancient prohibition of *omertà*? In the subject matter of their Mafia films, which represents only a few films out of their vast and accomplished canon, Scorsese and Coppola did little more than capitalize on a well-established, popular genre in

American films, the gangster movie. In other words, they discovered in their Italian experiences something that applied well to their larger society. Is this what we mean by assimilation? Can we discredit an artist for seizing an opportunity, even though it means leaving the values of the old neighborhood behind or because the Italian American artist tells something about us that we do not like?

In one sense, I would agree with the ideological implications of Mangione/Morreale's position. I, too, would like to see all Italian American artists speak only "from the world of the early immigrants," that socialist-labor point of view that created unions, such as the local Teamsters chapter that my father founded in Fresno, which gave Italian immigrants secure jobs and allowed them to raise families and educate their children throughout the 1950s and 60s. Those were the times of a heady idealism and a sense of hope for the future. Would this point of view then require us to censor the accomplishments of successful businessmen such as Lee Iacocca or Republican congressmen Alphonse D'Amato because they are not necessarily pro-labor? Do they lack social awareness? Rather, haven't all successful Italian Americans fulfilled the dream that was, indeed, located at the very center of "the world of the early immigrants"?

Finally, there is one more issue that *La Storia* raises. Italian American scholarship has yet to document fully the experience of Italians in the West. Though we have Andrew Rolle's seminal study, *The Immigrant Upraised*, the West, specifically California, is badly neglected. The authors do not mention what little research has been done, not even in the bibliography. Not only is *L'Italo-Americano* and its eighty-five year history in Los Angeles not mentioned in the text, it is not even listed as one of America's existing Italian newspapers in the bibliography. This suggests that the current, outdated model – mainly eastern and urban – used to define the ethnic experience has created gaps in our research and blind spots in our point of view. What does not fit the model is not relevant or does not exist as a legitimate subject of research.

The authors also missed a golden opportunity to extend that Italian immigrant political tradition, exemplified by the radicalism and prosecution of Sacco and Vanzetti, to the post-war period and to the West Coast. They failed to mention the leader of the national student usprising begun in the early 1960s at Berkeley and led by the son of Sicilian immigrants, Mario Savio. He represents a link from that "world of the early immigrants" to post-Vietnam America. Savio and the student movement he inspired all across America in the 1960s continue to influence our society today.

Savio inspired his generation in the same manner that Sacco and Vanzetti became the *cause célèbre* of the leftist movement during the Depression. He also suffered for the cause. In the end, Savio was persecuted for his outspoken leadership and high idealism. He was unjustly expelled from Berkeley in the 1970s, thus truncating a brilliant career in physics. He returned to the California State University system in the early 1980s to graduate *summa cum laude* in physics. Thereafter, he lived a quiet, private life, with only occasional speaking engagements, and taught secondary school in northern California, until his untimely death in November of 1996.

The omissions in *La Storia* by no means lessen its value. Rather, like any good historical study, *La Storia* informs us of the current state of Italian studies and points out areas that require further research and writing.

The Lore of the Folk

FROM ITALY TO NORTH AMERICA

Italian American Folklore
by Frances M. Malpezzi and William M. Clements

Malpezzi and Clements inform us in their introduction that one of the first works on Italian American folklore – *Southern Italian Folkways in Europe and America* – was written in 1938 as a handbook for social workers, medical personnel, and teachers. Current studies of Italian folkways go beyond practical manuals and tell us about social cohesion in North American Italian communities and what traditions have continued in the postwar period.

Written by two eminent folklorists, *Italian American Folklore* is a study of Italian American folk culture, from its origins to transplantation in America. In their ten chapters, the authors describe the raw material that has informed the narratives of writers from Pietro di Donato in the 1930s to Eugene Mirabelli's novels in the 1990s and in film from the silent era to the works of Scorsese, Coppola, and John Turturro, specifically his little-known but remarkable *Mac*. In *Italian American Folklore* we find the basis for not only group identity but the seed ground for high art.

Italian American Folklore describes the cultural patterns that have formed the mainstream of Italian American life over the last one hundred years. Chapter I, "Setting the Scene," begins with the Great Migration at the turn of this century. The authors write that

"Italians from both the north and south transplanted a rich cultural heritage, much of which had developed and was maintained without the support of official institutions of church or state." Their task was complicated, however, by the North/South split in Italian culture. In Centreville, Iowa, the authors report, the "Piedmontesi left the city and went to live . . . away from the Sicilians."

But such regional divisiveness does not prevent the authors from creating a coherent cultural fabric of Italian American life. In "Conversation," they document the development of that all too familiar hybrid of Italian/English that immigrants – to the chagrin of Italian-language purists – created: "*ais crima* (ice cream), *sanguiccio* (sandwich), *sonamagogna* (son of a gun)." In an earlier generation anyone who needed toilet facilities knew how to ask for the *baccausa*. In "Customs: The Life Cycle," the authors document the rituals related to births, baptisms, weddings, and funerals. Mothers had to be on guard against malocchio for their newborns, and the obligatory candy-coated almonds were served at weddings to ensure a fertile union.

In "The Traditional Calendar," the authors look at celebrations, from Sunday mass to religious and community festivals. The five chapters that follow explore "Folk Supernaturalism," "Folk Medicine," "Recreation and Games," "Stories and Story Telling," and "Drama, Music, and Dance." In the chapter on the most enduring Italian folkway, "Foodways," the authors discuss the centrality of food to Italian identity. As one immigrant reported, "as the years went on, while they [Italians] accepted other American ways and things, their food preferences always remained Italian." The authors point out, too, the significance of a garden for a generation of impoverished immigrant Italians who had little land to cultivate in the Old World.

This work illustrates how folkways enhanced Italian American identity in older communities and continue to solidify group identity in the post-war period. But what I also find significant about folklore studies is how parochial folkways continue to influence formal expressions in Italian American writing and film where Italian social cohesion and identity need to be articulated in scene and character.

Studies in Italian American Folklore
edited by Luisa Del Giudice

Born in Terracina, Italy, Luisa Del Giudice received her M.A. at the University of Toronto before finishing her Ph.D. at UCLA. She has done extensive research on Italian folklife in Los Angeles. Her current collection of six essays, *Studies in Italian American Folklore*, focuses on genres and regional influences of Italian culture in both Canada and the United States. The interesting aspect of Del Giudice's collection is that it documents the legacy of Italian folkways in two countries, America and Canada. In spite of the otherwise regional focus of the individual essays, each study expresses what Robert Viscusi calls elsewhere the "Italian commonwealth" and what Antonio D'Alfonso calles *aterritorial identity*, the dispersal of Italian culture through immigration. Del Giudice's collection documents a small part of the results of over a hundred years of Italian immigration throughout the world where Italian culture has been exported.

In the first essay, "Tears of Blood," Anna L. Chairetakis examines the style and form of the Calabrian *villanella*. In 1975 she recorded a group of women in the basement of a church in Brooklyn. She gives examples of the evolution of the form in both dialect and English and discusses the social context of this widely-used poetic form. In "The 'Archvilla,'" Del Giudice studies the evolution of the arch in residential and commercial architecture designed by Italian immigrants in Toronto, Canada. Where there were arches, there were Italians. She studies the arch's historical roots and social context as a "cultural representation" for Italians in Toronto. In "Playing With Food," Sabina Magliocco studies the role of food and Italian identity in festivals in the Italian American community of Clinton, Indiana. In her article, "From the *Paese* to the *Patria*," Dorothy Noyes studies the pilgrimage of a group of Italians in 1929 to Rome where they met Benito Mussolini. Through this event Prof. Noyes explains the significance of group membership for Italians and the role of the patronage system in Italian culture. In the last two essays, Paola Schellenbaum and Joseph Sciorra study in separate essays Italians in Northern California and a grotto dedicated to the Virgin in Staten Island. Sciorra studies the grotto as an expression of vernacular architecture that the Italian American community invested "with meaning through expressive behavior, the spoken word, and the written text."

Both the Malpezzi/Clements' and Del Giudice's books are significant contributions to an understanding of the Italian American folk narrative. However, neither work addresses the implications of change. How important are the forms of the older generation's beliefs, social rituals, and religious icons to younger generations? Whatever the specific changes that might have occurred in cultural patterns since, say, the 1960s, one place to look for the influence of Italian American folk culture is in the literature that North American Italians have published in the last forty years. For sociologists, folk culture is a social science to be studied; for the North American Italian writer, folklore is grist for the imagination. Ultimately, it is in poetry and fiction that we find both the meaning behind folk custom and the tensions that arise in a later generation's response to the folkways and values that their immigrant forebears brought to North America.

Italian Folktales in America:
The Verbal Art of an Immigrant Woman
by Elizabeth Mathias and Richard Raspa

Italian Folktales in America is a collection of folktales told by Clementina Todesco and recorded by her daughter, Bruna. In 1941, while she was studying folklore in college, Bruna Todesco recorded the folktales her mother had told her as a child. Her mother and father immigrated to America in the 1930s from Faller in northern Italy. Shortly before her death in 1961, Bruna deposited the collection of stories in the university archives. The stories were forgotten until 1974 when a university archivist discovered them.

As Roger Abrahams explains in his introduction to the work, it was the custom in Faller for the villagers to meet in the evenings at one of the villager's stables, a place that "was like a comfortable family room" where all the villagers could socialize and exchange information. Abrahams tells us that these gatherings of the men, women, and children of the village centered around an activity called the *filo*, the spinning of hemp. The adults told folktales for the general entertainment of everyone. The *filo* became for the villagers a social ritual in which the young smembers of the community not only learned practical skills, but also the requisite social and moral values of the village as well.

Clementina possessed an extraordinary memory. Bruna recorded in great detail the stories that her mother recalled from her childhood. Mathias and Raspa did an additional ten years research on the social background in Faller and Clementina's personal history, which compose two separate sections in the volume. The stories that Clementina told fell into two categories: the *märchen* tales, historical tales that have their basis in the oral tradition; and legends and religious stories. The tales are relatively simple and fall into familiar folktale patterns. But most important, all the stories end with a clearly defined moral.

In "Barbarina and the Black Snake," Barbarina's steadfastness and perseverance are challenged by a promise she has made to a prince who had been turned into an ugly snake by his wicked aunt. In the end of the story the moral is clear: you must sometimes endure hardship before you are rewarded. In "The Cats Under the Sea," Maria is mistreated by her evil stepmother, who always favors her biological but lazy daughter. After Maria goes under water to a place called Catdom, the king of Catdom rewards her and later punishes her slovenly half-sister. In a similar story, "The Cherry Tree and Pumpkin Vine," a stepdaughter is sent away from home by her evil stepmother, but she is eventually rewarded for her virtue. The Stepmother and her biological daughter suffer a horrible fate. In "The Dark Men," included in the nine tales in the section entitled *Legends and Religious Tales,* a husband kills his pious wife who goes directly to heaven while her husband is dismembered by the devil and cast into hell. Similarly, in "The Old Man and the Rosary," a young boy scoffs at his pious elders and is nearly carried off by the devil.

Interestingly, there is a personal dimension to the stories that Clementina chose to recall, especially those relating to the evil stepmother. Apparently she was raised by a selfish stepmother who favored her biological children over Clementina and her siblings. For Clementina there was even a day of reckoning when she returned to Italy in her later years and confronted her aged stepmother, who was well aware of the evil she had done and fearful of her day of judgment.

Italian Folktales is an interesting and valuable contribution to the field of ethnography. However, there is one curious omission. The editors do not mention or list in their bibliography Italo Calvino's *Italian Folktales*, which is the most important and comprehensive collection of Italian folktales in English and Italian. In an interesting way, Calvino's collection, composed of folktales from Italy's various regions, provides further context for Clementina's stories. Calvino's folktales, unlike the Brothers Grimm's or Hans Christian Andersen's stories, have not been sanitized for young readers or a general audience. While Calvino's collection does contain tales like Clementina's that imply a well-ordered universe, many suggest a view of experience that is unpredictable and hostile.

Clementina's tales, by contrast, are clear and well organized. Each narrative is relentless in its progression from the first incident to the predictable, unambiguous moral. Taken as a whole, Clementina's twenty-two tales represent a society of people who held well-defined beliefs and no doubt lived in what they felt was a well-ordered, just, and predictable universe. Not only do her stories speak volumes about Clementina's life in her Northern Italian village, they also suggest to us both the values and the expectations that immigrants brought to America with them. Steadfastness and perseverance were joined with the expectation of social justice in America. These values shaped immigrants' attitudes toward their harsh working conditions and influenced the direction of their personal lives in North America. These same values continue to shape the form and content of the fiction and poetry that is being written about their lives by succeeding generations. While the oral tradition that Clementina's stories represent may be gone, the values that her recorded stories express endure in the North American narrative that is being written today.

Understanding the Present

FROM THE VILLAGE TO THE SUBURBS

The Italians of Greenwich Village
by Donald Tricarico

The story that Donald Tricarico tells in *The Italians of Greenwich Village* is one among many studies that have been written over the last thirty-five years. Though Tricarico's study is an original contribution to Italian studies in North America, it is typical of a whole genre of works that American university scholars have produced on Italians in North America, from Chicago, Missouri, Texas, Rochester, Montreal, Oklahoma, and New York to Italians in the West. Each of these many works is an important chapter in the role that Italian immigrants and their offspring have played in the settlement and development of urban centers and small rural towns throughout North America.

There is something engaging about works like Tricarico's. Approaching such studies, the reader anticipates the possible discovery of something personal, such as a family name in another Italian settlement in America. But, more important, there is too a sense of awe in finding that the experience that one had in an Italian neighborhood in a small town in Texas or California was repeated all over North America. The parochialism that is often attached to "minority" culture suddenly vanishes in the face of the broad base of the Italian immigrant experience throughout society if not the world. In Robert Viscusi's words in *The Columbus People*, there is a commonwealth of

"Little Italies" that are "borne of Large Italy." This is Italy dispersed.

It is not surprising that the reader is able to anticipate even before opening a work such as Donald Tricarico's how the story will end. The first generation settles into Little Italies. Then the third and fourth generations, based on the hard work and success of their forebears, abandon the urban neighborhoods for the suburbs. They leave only a few of the aged behind in the old neighborhoods that are undergoing yet another face-lift by the influx of a new group of urban dwellers. There are those familiar images which haunt works like Tricarico's of aged Italians who cling tenaciously to their turf: their old apartments, cafes, or favorite restaurants. This is a pattern since the 1960s.

Between the initial settlement of the immigrant Italian community and its final transformation, Tricarico's well-researched chapters explore the details of Italian American life in Greenwich Village before 1980. In these chapters we find not only a description of a particular Italian community, but the documentation of that generic, universal experience shared by all Italian immigrants and their offspring.

As Tricarico explains, the family served as the basic unit in the lives of the new immigrants, including the extended family of relatives. Complementing the values being taught in the home was the closely controlled "family neighborhood." Tricarico writes that "neighbors cooperated with one another to assure that the cultural blueprint outlined by the home was being followed." In other words, neighbors looked out for the interests of other families.

Beyond the neighborhood, the social structure of the new immigrant community offered a variety of mutual aid societies that served the immigrants and aided them in their transition into life in America. From the "family neighborhood" developed the social neighborhood, which contained a variety of private clubs and associations. The men in the neighborhood usually belonged to these private clubs. While not confined exclusively to the home, women's activities still revolved around their traditional roles as home-makers and mothers. The neighborhood parish and district politics were two other important social groups that influenced directly the quality of life in the neighborhood. Organized crime is another element that Tricarico examines in the neighborhood social structure.

With the renaming of a section of the south village SoHo (south of Houston) in 1971 and the influx of artists and upper-class residents, the character of the Italian community in the Village changed radically. Though the Italian neighborhood was only on the border of the area renamed SoHo by the city, apartment rents began to soar and the commercial face of the neighborhood began to change. As the young moved out, the vacuum they left was filled by the new residents. The parish changed, as did all of the social organizations, and the area became a "neighborhood of strangers." Gone was the old "family neighborhood."

Before and since Tricarico's work there has been a plethora of studies documenting the lives, work, social organizations, and religious practices of immigrants and their offspring in both urban and rural America. Robert F. Foerster's ground breaking volume, *The Italian Emigration of Our Times* (1919), was among the first works to study Italian immigration worldwide. Among the most recent studies worth mentioning are Michael La Sorte's *La Merica: Images of Italian Greenhorn Experience*, Colleen Lehy Johnson's *Growing Up and Growing Old in Italian American Families*, Adria Bernardi's *Houses With Names: The Italian Immigrants of Highwood, Illinois*, Salvatore LaGumina's *From Steerage to Suburb: Long Island Italians*, and Andrew Rolle's *The Immigrant Upraised*, which focuses on Italians in the West.

In the late 1960s and the early 1970s, there was great concern on the part of some sociologists that something valuable and irreplaceable was being lost by the transformation of our urban ethnic neighborhoods. In fact, in the 1980s Richard Alba's provocative study, *Italian Americans: Into the Twilight of Ethnicity*, made perhaps the most significant impact on the questions surrounding not just Italian American identity, but the continued existence of Italian Americans as a distinct cultural entity in the future. Alba's study is addressed perceptively by several scholars in *The Columbus People*, "Italian Identity and Ethnicity in North America." Scholars seem to agree on one level that the old models of ethnicity are no longer adequate. Yet the current model that identifies Italian ethnicity only with the early twentieth-century urban immigrant experience has not yet been replaced with a more diverse definition of Italian culture in North America. Rolle's study of Italians in the West, *The Immigrant Upraised*, suggests some possible alternatives. In Canada, Filippo Salvatore has argued persuasively for a critical approach that redines the boundaries of North American Italian literature.

What Tricarico's and Alba's studies tell us is that what we see in our ethnic communities is change, not necessarily dissolution or decline. The establishment of Italian cultural associations, like the National Italian American Foundation, *Arba Sicula*, and the many new Italian cultural groups throughout the country, demonstrate that the old neighborhood and its nexus of social organizations has now been resurrected in another form. Besides, how do we explain, in the wake of the dissolution of the old urban neighborhood, a veritable renaissance in North American Italian writing over the last three decades? Viscusi suggests that the commonwealth of "Little Italies" has become a commonwealth without specific urban, geographical boundaries: a commonwealth of shared Italian culture. In Pasquale Verdicchio's terms, post-colonial deterritorialization has resulted in "a site of reterritorialization" of Italians in North America: an "histroical bloc" of shared culture. Tricarico's book, and all the others like it, tell the Americans of Italian descent where they have come from. With the advantage of such well-researched works on Italians in America, we are now better able to assess where we are going. Currently, we have only one model, that of immigration and settlement in urban settings. If these studies represent the twilight of ethnicity, as Alba suggests, then new models of ethnicity must be created to explain the new ethnicity for the twenty-first century.

Struggle and Success: An Anthology of the Italian Immigrant Experience in California
edited by Paola A. Sensi-Isolani and Phylis Cancilla Martinelli

Largely because of the concentration of Italian immigrants in northeastern urban centers at the turn of the century, over the last thirty years most of the scholarship on Italian Americans has focused on the eastern urban experience. An important deviation from that pattern was Andrew Rolle's *The Immigrant Upraised* (1968), which was the first study in English of Italians in the West. Unfortunately, since Rolle's groundbreaking work, not many scholars have followed his lead. When they have, too often their research has been aimed at the predictable areas of San Francisco and, to a lesser degree, California's Central Coast. Alan Balboni, however, broke new ground in his *Beyond the Mafia: Italian Americans and the Development of Las Vegas*, which documents Italians' contributions to the development of Las Vegas, in the casinos and professions.

Broader in scope, *Struggle and Success*, a collection of ten essays, represents some of the best research that has been done so far on the experiences and contributions of Italians in California. However, before I look at the content of the essays, I would like to suggest several major areas of Italian American life in California that have gone unnoticed by scholars.

Absent in *Struggle and Success* is any research on Italians in the Salinas Valley, San Joaquin Valley, and Pomona Valley in the west end of San Bernardino County. To their credit, in their

Conclusion, the editors mention that more work needs to be done in Fresno, which has been host to a thriving Italian community for more than a hundred years. From the outset of the settlement of the San Joaquin Valley in the nineteenth century, Italian Americans have been a significant force in valley farming, food processing, and food distribution. Over the generations Italians have been central to the food processing and packing industry, from fresh fruits and vegetables to processed fruits such as figs and raisins. There are no studies on Jewish and Italian produce brokers who distributed fresh fruits and vegetables from valley farms and packing houses to the Los Angeles and New York produce markets. If historians are looking for studies on cross-cultural relations in this era of multiculturalism, this could be an area of fecund research.

A significant part of the San Joaquin Valley history is the development of labor unions in the 1930s in the packing industry. This was an era of active and often violent unionization. Both my parents were instrumental in establishing the Teamsters Union in their fig and olive plant in Fresno. Other plants in Fresno unionized at the same time. What role did Italians play in general in this important movement in Fresno and the valley? Even more important, a large percentage of the work force in area plants was comprised of women who did piece work on the packing lines. Without the cooperation of the women – including many different ethnic groups besides Italians – there would have been no unions. In this era of feminist reevaluation of the contributions of women to society, there are great opportunities here to explore the role of women in the establishment of unions in the valley. Nothing can be more important to a stable family life than working women and men – husbands and wives – who walked picket lines to raise their salaries and make their jobs more secure.

Virtually unexplored is the role of Italian immigrant farmers in both the San Joaquin and Salinas Valleys. Are there cross-cultural studies possible, say, between Mexican, Armenian, and Italian farmers? What is the relationship here between farmers and laborers? There is a great deal more research possible in areas other than the well-known Di Georgio/Chavez historic battle.

Another area that has not been studied is the role of Italian men and women in the canning industry, from Fresno to Hollister, Gilroy, Salinas, Monterey, San Jose, Oakdale, Turlock, and Modesto. My mother made this circuit with her sisters and immigrant mother for nearly two decades. Again this is a fecund area of research on the role of immigrant women and their daughters in this industry. The canning was done exclusively by women, while the men did the heavy work. More studies also have to be done on the ownership of the canneries in these areas. What was the relationship between Italian immigrant owners and their Italian immigrant workers?

Another area that is absent in Italian American studies is the Pomona Valley. The now defunct Kaiser Steel Mill in Fontana had a significant Italian labor force drawn from the Italian communities in Ontario and Upland. Before World War II, Cucamonga – now known as Rancho Cucamonga – was the major wine producing area of the United States. The west end of San Bernardino County boasted more than forty wineries, the vast majority owned by Italians. Italians, as well, owned all of the vineyards, only a fraction of which remain today. Secondo Guasti rivaled the wine production of Italian Swiss Colony in northern California. Today, the Filippi and Galeano wineries, among the oldest in the state, are still family owned and operated.

A little known fact is that because of its large Italian population, Cucamonga was the site of an Italian prisoner of war camp during World War II. On Sundays area residents, some from as far away as Los Angeles, would drive to Cucamonga to visit the camp and would bring the Italian soldiers home for dinner. Some of the prisoners married and remained in the area after the war.

Aside from these understandable omissions, the twelve articles in *Struggle and Success* are a valuable contribution to Italian studies. In section one, Historical Perspective, Joseph Giovinco's article, "Success in the Sun," studies the progress of Italians, mainly in northern California, during the progressive era. Paola A. Sensi-Isolani's article, "Tradition and Transition in a California Paese," is a study of Italians in Sonoma County. Of special note is Rosalind Giardina Crosby's extremely valuable article on "The Italians of Los Angeles."

Section two, Occupations and Economic Life, contains informative articles on A. P. Giannini by Felice Bonadio and on Andrea Sbarboro, the founder of Italian-Swiss Colony, by Deanna Paoli Gumina. William Richardson's article on "The Fishermen of San Diego: The Italians" is especially valuable and suggests the possibilities of more research. Elizabeth Reis' article focuses on the cannery workers of northern California. In section three, *Social and Political Experience*, the articles focus on entertainment, education, and Americanization of San Francisco Italians. Stephen Fox's article on "The Relocation of Italian Americans During World War II" is a chapter from his work on the internment of Italians during the war. The last section, *The Immigrant Community*, concludes with articles on Italians in Los Angeles' Lincoln Heights by Gilbert Gonzalez and the Italians of the Excelsior district of San Francisco by Phylis Cancilla Martinelli.

Struggle and Success is an invaluable piece of scholarship on the Italian American experience. However, a great deal more research needs to be done on the role of Italians in California history before we can accurately assess Italians' contributions to the cultural, economic, and social life in America.

ITALIAN AMERICAN WRITERS

Christ in Concrete
by Pietro di Donato

Pietro di Donato, the son of an Italian immigrant, was born on April 3, 1911. He grew up in West Hoboken, New Jersey. His father, an Italian immigrant, was a bricklayer and was killed on a construction site. His father's death became the basis of di Donato's first novel, *Christ in Concrete*, the most celebrated work by an Italian American written before World War II. As Fred Gardaphé writes in the Introduction, "While critics disagreed as to the novel's formal merits, they unanimously concurred that a major voice had broken into the American literary scene" at the time of the novel's publication.

But di Donato's fame as a new, proletarian voice at the close of the Depression was short-lived. As Gardaphé points out, *Christ in Concrete* has only been reprinted once, in 1976, since its initial publication over fifty years ago. The novel began as a short story which appeared in *Esquire Magazine* in 1937 and was later chosen for the anthology of the *Best Short Stories of 1938*. Di Donato then expanded the story to a novel, which earned the remarkable distinction of being picked as a main selection of the 1939 Book-of-the-Month-Club over John Steinbeck's *The Grapes of Wrath*. As Chicago writer Studs Terkel explains in the Preface, *Christ in Concrete* "is a powerful contemporary novel. And while for too long novels of working class life have been out of fashion, the hard reality of our day makes them as pertinent and timely as ever."

Di Donato directs his wrath at the construction company that sends his main character, Geremio, to his death and at the indifferent investigating governmental bureaucracy which refuses to indict the company for its misdeeds. On the job, the men are dehumanized by their working conditions. Di Donato's style is often a cascade of words and run-on sentences: "The men are transformed into single, silent beasts. Snoutnose steamed through ragged mustache whiplashing sand into mixer Ashes-ass dragged under four-by-twelve beam Lean clawed wall knots jumping in jaws masonry crumbled dust billowed thundered choked . . ." The torrid pace of industrial America, captured by di Donato's style, dehumanizes the immigrant. They are trapped in an economic system that is indifferent to their plight and suffering .

One day Geremio and several of his Italian coworkers are entombed in concrete when the scaffolding they are working on collapses. To apply for welfare, Geremio's son Paul and his widow go to a government office and speak to a bureaucrat who asks if Geremio was an American citizen. When Paul admits that his father had only just taken out his papers, the bureaucrat answers definitively, "Well, then he wasn't a citizen." The case is closed.

Paul, like di Donato when his own father was killed in a similar mishap, has to go to work at a young age. While working, he faces the same indignities on the job that his father had endured. But what finally distances *Christ in Concrete* from other proletarian novels of the period is that it is also an intensely personal story. Like James T. Farrell and his treatment of the Chicago Irish, di Donato offers a harsh, critical appraisal not only of Depression-era, *laissez-faire* capitalism, but also of his roots as a Catholic. Paul undergoes a crisis of faith. The Church is depicted as indifferent to the plight of its people. After his appeal for welfare is denied, Paul goes to the rectory to ask Father John for assistance. Father John's insensitive response to Paul is to offer him a piece of cake from his abundant dinner to take home to his now fatherless family.

In the face of such indifference, from both industry and the Church, di Donato appeals to Italian workers to look to themselves and their families as a solution to the exploitation and indifference that they encounter in America. It is not hard to understand the derivation of such an ideological point of view in the Italian immigrant. This same appeal to community and family served for centuries as southern Italians' first line of defense against exploitative colonial governments and their allies in the Church .

Christ in Concrete remains as extraordinary today as it was in the year it was published. It is an important novel that dramatizes, in both its style and content, the urban plight of Italian immigrants in North America. It ranks with the works of Anzia Yezierska's and Abraham Cahan's works that document the plight of Jewish immigrants in urban America before World War II.

Calabrian Tales and *From Behind a Chair*
by Vito Aieta

Calabrian Tales is a collection of short stories, all of which are set in the fictional village of Marina, located on the western coast of Calabria. The village is very much like Fuscaldo where Aieta was born and lived as a child before his immigration to America. After coming to America before World War II, Aieta spent the rest of his life in Cincinnati, where he worked as a beautician, which became the setting for his second volume of stories, *From Behind a Chair.*

The belated and self-published appearance of these two collections is an example of how Italian American writing has largely remained on the margins in American publishing. Aieta remains virtually unknown, even among Italian American critics. Not the product of a university graduate writing program, Aieta instead went to school in the fiction of the great Sicilian writer Luigi Pirandello. His stories are seminal expressions of the immigrant experience. He explores the nature and meaning of the bicultural experience that he lived between his village, Fuscaldo, in Calabria and in Cincinnati in the years before and shortly after World War II. Making frequent trips back to his place of birth, Aieta maintained contact with southern Italy. With his roots still deep in Calabrian life and culture, in *From Behind a Chair* he brings a unique perspective to narcissistic American culture. In *Calabrian Tales* "La Merica" becomes the abstract icon of Aieta's Calabrian characters' collective dream to escape their sorrowful fate in their isolated, southern Italian village. As in Pirandello's stories and plays, fate, vanity, and a profound sense of limitations affect the lives of Aieta's characters in his stories.

In "The Empty Train," Aieta writes that the people of Marina "are always making something out of nothing so they can forget the harsh reality of their way of life." The fishermen of the village tell of an apparition that they see each year: a woman who appears to them wrapped in a veil with her long hair flowing in the wind. The story becomes for all the villagers a symbol of their dreams and also of their limitations, especially for one villager, Angelo Attavio. He falls in love with a young woman, Aurora. But like the chimera that appears to the fishermen, she is equally elusive and impossible to grasp for Angelo. In the end of the story she goes back to a former lover. Crushed, Angelo leaves Marina for another town.

In "The Piazza," the narrator of the story returns to Marina after many years spent in America. He becomes reacquainted with an old friend, Beppe, a former prize fighter, who has lost his dream of happiness and fame. Just before he was to have had a title fight in America, he was deported back to his small native village, where he languishes in poverty and obscurity. He can only dream of his lost opportunities. Similarly, in one of the best stories in the volume, "Cavalier," Francesco Saracino, a poor street sweeper, yearns to have the respect of his fellow villagers, his only goal in life. But one day his wife cuckolds him. In typical fashion, the villagers mock him for his wife's behavior, and when he finds that he is unable to kill his wife's lover and have his revenge, he loses all hope of ever regaining the respect of the village. He resigns himself to his low status in life as a street sweeper and an errand boy.

In the other nine stories in the volume, Aieta's characters more often than not fail to realize their dreams. Out of Aieta's immigrant experience come characters who live bifurcated lives, caught between the harsh reality of southern Italian life and their dreams of escape, either to abstract and idealized "La Merica" or to some equally improbable idealized notion.

The nine stories in *From Behind a Chair* are set in a beauty parlor, which serves Aieta well as a metaphor for our narcissistic American culture. In this setting, in which Aieta worked for most of his adult life, he explores the vanities and illusions that misguide his American characters. In the first story entitled "Juan," Mrs. Brown asks Enrico, the middle-aged character who ties all the stories together, to make her look young again. The beauty parlor is her fountain of youth and Enrico its high priest who is supposed to perform miracles. Mrs. Brown tells Enrico that she must look beautiful for her rich and famous husband, who takes her along on his many business trips. It becomes clear to Enrico that she is little more than a prop in her husband's successful business career. What she needs, Enrico concludes, is someone to love her, not the artificiality of a new hair style nor the role of a mannequin in her husband's career aspirations.

Similarly, in "Every Year One Day," Maura Paprin has been wearing the same hair style for twenty-five years because that is the way her husband liked it. Now that he is dead, Maura comes to Enrico with a photograph of a ridiculous hair style, "a hair-do like Norma Shearer's in Marie Antoniette." Enrico thinks to himself as he works over her, "she wasn't the only one who tried to live in a reality which time has made almost devoid of all meaning." In a magical twist to the story, Enrico sees her that evening, and she is youthful and beautiful. But at the stroke of twelve, her aged, wrinkled skin and the palsied twitch of her left arm return. Maura's transformation was illusory and fleeting.

Though separate in setting, both books are linked thematically. The disappointed dreams and hopes of his Calabrian characters mirror the desire for eternal youth of his American characters. They are certain to grow old, just as his Calabrian characters will never escape their *distino*, the perennial disappointments they face in their impoverished village. As the immigrant "other" in American culture, Aieta perceptively captures the vanity of the American character. As an exile from Italian culture, he looks back in his Calabrian stories and depicts the stagnation of village life. Time has not only stopped, but history as well seems to have bypassed the lives of his southern Italian characters.

The World at Noon
by Eugene Mirabelli

The World at Noon is a generational novel, but it is not written in the usual epic, pulp-fiction form. Eugene Mirabelli, who has written three previous novels, is too good a writer for that. He has a exceptional ability to meld the fabulous and the real, to capture a sense of place and time but not leave the reader mired only in the temporal and mundane.

The novel is about five generations of the Cavallù/Pellegrino families. It takes us from Calabria and Sicily of the nineteenth century to contemporary America. Great grandfather Angelo Cavallù was born with the flanks of a horse. On his wedding night in 1860 in Carco, Sicily, he so terrifies his innocent young wife, Ava, when she sees his flanks that she vows never to sleep with him. But Angelo reassures her that any woman who sleeps with him inherits, among other things, eternal beauty.

On the other side of the family, great grandmother Stella DiMare is a goddess of incomparable beauty. As a young woman she lived and worked, befitting both her great beauty and low social class, in the Conca d'Oro bordello in Reggio, Calabria. When Franco Morrelli from Cosenza visits the Conca d'Oro one evening in 1860, he is so smitten with Stella's goddess-like beauty, he proposes to her on the spot. But before she accepts, Stella demands that Franco must pass one test to prove to her and himself that he is truly in love with her.

In addition to Angelo's wedding-night revelation to his bride, the story is filled with other fabulous events. Years after Stella's death, her equally beautiful daughter Marianna on her death bed glimpses Stella's apparition, like Botticelli's Venus, beckoning to her from a large scallop shell just off shore in the sea. In a foreshadowing of Marianna's vision, Stella had told Franco when they met in the bordello in 1860, "The people of southern Italy never made much of a difference between mortals and gods, and you never knew when a man might become a god, or a goddess becomes a woman, or vice versa." Even the red-shirted Garibaldi, whom Franco served under during the liberation of Italy, blesses children and is "greeted as a god" by his admirers. Mirabelli intertwines these atavistic non-chronological chapters of gods, demi-gods, and Italians with their contemporary descendants, Nicolo and Maeve Pellegrino.

La storia – both American and Italian history – plays an important part in shaping Nicolo's character. Nicolo spent his youth in America on the East Coast. As a boy he and his parents lived in a coach house that overlooked a cemetery where he and his friends played. It contained the graves and headstones of the earliest Anglo-American settlers of the New World: the Hastings, Fisks, Childs, and Estabrooks. In America, Mirabelli's de-

scendants of Italian immigrants live in an ambiguous relationship with the icons of American history.

As a young man Nicolo attended the long-established
bastions of Anglo-American culture, MIT and Harvard. His
haunts as a college student and after are Cambridge, Boston,
Gloucester, and other parts of New England. In all of these
chapters Mirabelli evokes a strong sense of place. After his
graduation from college and wearing "a dazzling seersucker
suit," he visits his Aunt Regina, his mother's sister, in
Gloucester. While there, his thirty-something aunt seduces
him, and they become involved in a protracted affair. We are
reminded here of Nicolo's centaur-like great grandfather Angelo Cavallù. Regina, like the women who descended from the
mythical Stella DiMare, is as uncommonly beautiful as her
appetite for her virile nephew is unquenchable.

When Nicolo had first seen Maeve in college, he was
smitten with her beauty: "her green eyes, high cheek bones,
and hair like a long black banner." Nicolo says that "she sank
into my heart like an ax." Not only is she beautiful, like all the
women in the family, her past, too, is the stuff of legend. Her
name is derived from Maeve of Connacht, the Irish Queen,
who, as legend has it, was no mere mortal. Even for the Irish
Maeve, history is the template for her character. When she first
saw Nicolo, her "heart was a cinder." Before she and even
Nicolo realized it, he proposed and they were married. We
think here of the passion that coupled Stella and Franco.

Like his father, Nicolo became a scholar. In their salad
days in the 1960s, Maeve and Nicolo traveled west and thought
that they would live off yogurt, fruit, and herb tea. Starvation
did not suit them. They finally returned to the East and settled
an hour from Boston, where we find them, twenty-six years
and three children into their troubled marriage. Nicolo teaches
in Boston and Maeve, her beauty and wit as undiminished as
the day Nicolo met her, runs a desktop publishing business. It's
a good life, full of the bounty that America promises to all

immigrants and their offspring. But a tension develops, unspoken, between the twentieth-century descendants of those legendary gods and goddesses of southern Italy and Ireland and their mundane life lived in modern America.

At mid-life, Maeve and Nicolo are not entirely content with their lives. Nicolo meets and falls in love with Roxane, his daughter's twenty-something friend. Maeve also has a beau, Felix Stout, a pontificating, self-proclaimed romantic who is a monumental bore. But she is not merely retaliating against her wayward husband. We learn that before Felix, years before, just after the birth of their third and last child, there was also Father John Sullivan. When alone and away from the men in her life, including Nicolo, Maeve feels that she can and must be herself. These are the only times when she feels truly whole. When the children are off to school and Nicolo is away at the university, she says, "I am free to be myself, alone and by myself." With abandon, she undresses and strolls naked through the quiet rooms of the empty house.

Maeve is not blind, nor is Felix Stout's constant presence at the Pellegrino home lost upon Nicolo. Both Maeve and Nicolo look across an abyss at each other, attempting to comprehend their actions and to sort out their conflicting emotions and loyalties. Maeve doesn't suspect; she knows, just as Nicolo knows, without being told about Felix Stout.

But Nicolo is troubled by his infidelity. He feels that he is committing an historical transgression, as much as a personal violation, in his infidelity. His past hovers about him in strange and curious ways throughout the novel. Like Marianna who glimpses her long-deceased mother, Nicolo sees apparitions of his dead father regularly, often happy and well dressed. At his daughter's wedding in the end of the novel, he sees the apparitions of his father and of his long-deceased grandmother seated at a table and enjoying the family gathering. The past hovers about Nicolo and obliquely speaks to him of his past and his own mortality.

In the end, Nicolo and Maeve come down to earth, so to speak. Their love is rekindled and sense of family is restored. One night when Felix and Roxane leave Nicolo's and Maeve's lives for good, Nicolo remembers a time when all the family was together at home, and Nicolo thinks, "I knew I had them all in one fleet, together and safe. And I was happy." The past and kinship ultimately win out over his and Maeve's struggle to be totally free.

Mirabelli's prose is robust and daring. He takes risks with his copious sentences, as he does with his fabulous demi-god characters, that leave you breathless. In a sentence his characters cast a shadow; in a passage he evokes time and place. *The World at Noon* is history, myth, and folklore. But, above all else, it is art. It is a perfect melding of the past and present and demonstrates the great possibilities that bicultural writing brings to North America.

Umbertina
by Helen Barolini

When I finished *Umbertina* I had the feeling that I had read a novel that has the rare quality of being both epic in its scope and yet lyrical in its style. Helen Barolini's novel focuses on the lives of three women, from the 1860s to the 1970s. The first third of the novel centers on the immigrant experiences of Umbertina and her large family. In the last two thirds of the novel Barolini turns to the lives of Umbertina's granddaughter, Marguerite, and her great granddaughter, Tina. The novel, though not long, covers four generations of Italian Americans. At the same time, Barolini is able to develop the nuances that shape the consciousness of her three characters as women and as Americans with Italian roots.

Umbertina is a groundbreaking story about what it means to be an Italian American woman in post-war America. Compared with its predecessors in the Italian American novel, *Umbertina* brings a greater psychological depth to the bicultural experience. Barolini's women, especially Marguerite and her daughter Tina, exemplify the dilemmas faced by Italian women suspended between two cultures, neither of which is willing to give women an equal place in the social order.

Part one of the novel begins in the village of Castagna, Calabria, from which Umbertina Longobardi and her husband, Serafino, emigrate to America. Not long after their arrival on the East Coast, she and Serafino work their way out of New York's Lower East Side and move to upstate New York where they prosper in the retail grocery and wholesale business. Umbertina is a strong woman, stronger than her husband, in both will and constitution. She exhibits those characteristics that we have come to identify with those first Italian immigrants who settled America: strong willed, frugal, dedicated to family, and hard working. By the end of her life, though, Umbertina feels a sense of loss. An immigrant from the barren hills of Calabria, she had fought against nearly insurmountable odds in America. She raised children in the New World who knew nothing of hardship or poverty. As she reflects on her life, she feels herself an exile, even in the land she helped build. She is saddened by the fact that none of her grandchildren can communicate with her because none can speak Calabrese.

"She had won," Barolini writes, "but who could she tell the story to? At times the doubt came to her whether she really won, after all. All her life had been a struggle for family, and now in her old age she saw some signs that made her uneasy." Would the next generation perpetuate the values she had transplanted in the New World? Or would her family become materialistic and compromise the family values that had been the basis of their survival in Italy and success in America? She dies doubting her own accomplishments.

Part two focuses on the life of Marguerite Morosini. Freed, but only partially, from the social restrictions of her immigrant grandmother, Umbertina, Marguerite travels to Europe, where she has a series of affairs. Once in Italy, she meets and then marries the famous but older Italian writer, Alberto Morosini. They travel and live between Italy and America, have three children, and return in grief to Italy after the death of their son. Far from the storybook marriage she had imagined it to be, her life with Alberto is subsumed by his career. Famous literati surround her both in America and Italy. But they only see her as an appendage to her famous husband. She had traveled a long way, both geographically and emotionally, in her newly found freedom as an Italian American woman, only to discover that she is where she began and where her grandmother had always been as a woman. In her youth she lived with her father's admonishment that "it was not nice to look too Italian and to speak bad English ... Italians were not a serious people." He tells her, "We are Americans." As an adult and after her separation from Alfredo, with a failed marriage and without a career, she admonishes herself: she feels she is a "failure both as an American woman and as an Italian." Even with her new freedom, she cannot find succor anywhere. She travels to America and then rushes back to Florence: "She couldn't belong completely in the States any more and had never belonged completely in Europe." As a single woman, she can only feel "part of the permanently dispossessed." Without her husband she struggles to find her own identity. But her section ends in a lugubrious manner. She remains, in her associations with famous male writers, merely an appendage to Italian culture. Barolini concludes, "Nothing had changed" for Marguerite. Before it can, she is killed in a car accident.

In section three her daughter, Tina, raised in both Italy and America, is a young woman destined to resolve the bicultural dilemma that her mother had lived with all her life. Ivy-league educated, she is to the 1970s what her mother was in her freedom to her generation. Tina has a live-in boy friend, tosses the I Ching, and smokes pot. She has a recurring dream in which she is stuck at a crossroads in an unknown part of Italy. She sets out to resolve what her mother never could in her life. She returns to Calabria to find the origins of Umbertina and her own roots.

In the process, she reconciles herself with her hyphenated identity, which she once scorned. In her journey south to Calabria, she begins to identify more with her southern roots than with her father's Venetian origins. But when she arrives in Castagna, her experience is like so many Italian Americans who make the return visit. She is unsure of her place in the village: "more and more she seemed to herself an intruder." She has the sense that Umbertina wants her to return to America and to abandon her quest. When her trip to Calabria comes to an end, Umbertina appears an abstraction, still an elusive and ill-defined aspect of her personality.

Once in America, she tells her future husband, "Well, I guess we'll just hyphenate the kids." Ultimately, she begins to understand her divided self and reconciles the two halves of her identity. She finally understands what Umbertina means to her. To emigrate is to leave Italy behind, but the immigrant upon arrival, and for generations to come, retains a part of that culture and identity. This is what Tina learns about herself and about her mother's own failed quest for self-knowledge and identity as an Italian American woman.

Tina knows that she, a woman with strong roots in another class and place, does not belong to Castagna. At the same time, in the end, she feels closer to Umbertina and to a past that she realizes has shaped her character. Her dilemma, unlike her mother's and even Umbertina's, is reconciled.

Astoria
by Robert Viscusi

Robert Viscusi is Professor of English at Brooklyn College of the City University of New York. Well-known poet, essayist, and novelist, Viscusi has written illuminating studies on the influence of Italy in the works of such writers as William Shakespeare and English poet Robert Browning. He has, as well, made major contributions to Italian American studies.

A cross between a novel and a memoir, *Astoria* is an engaging and sometimes difficult work. Ultimately, we are asked to take it as a fictional account of its anonymous narrator's travels to Paris and Rome and his spiritual journey through European history and his own family past. As a play on words, the title expresses the major theme in the work, as well as a major theme in nearly all Italian American literature: history. Astoria is the narrator's Italian immigrant neighborhood in Queens, but, more important, it is also a play on the Italian *la storia* (history). Astoria is a specific, definable locale, with street names and boundaries, but it is also a word that suggests the history of the great migration from Europe. Astoria/*la storia* is a sign that resonates with the personal aspirations and the collective legends of millions of immigrant Italians.

Americans of Italian descent who remain close to the experience of the Great Migration carry Astoria/*la storia* in their heads, with all the complex and sometimes contradictory associations that we find in Viscusi's novel. The narrator moves from the parochial (Astoria) to the universal (*la storia*). He says in the opening of the novel as he travels to the heart of European civilization, "My journey no longer seemed to me my own expedition but rather the node or never-ending of what I knew to be a vast movement of people." In traveling to Europe he engages *la storia* at its roots, Paris, the site of the French Revolution, and Rome, the center of the Italian Risorgimento. These events in human history were pivotal points for European life.

Together the two revolutions freed the *borghese* from the limitations of the past. More important, the narrator explains, the Risorgimento, paradoxically, initiated the great migration of Italians that scattered them throughout the world.

While in Paris and Rome, the narrator experiences something he calls the Stendhal Syndrome, an epiphany. This could happen to anyone while standing before a great painting by Caravaggio or in the cavernous naves of one of Paris' or Rome's great churches. It happens to the narrator while he is standing in Les Invalides before Napoléon's tomb. In Paris he sees himself in the context of Astoria/*la storia*: as a product of all that is before him. Out of this insight he "weave[s] the texture of l'Astoria, a tapestry or photograph that must be, upon minute consideration, a dialogue of small distinctions." But the small distinctions of Astoria/*la storia*, like the minute gold and colored threads of a giant tapestry, serve ultimately to fashion larger, discernable patterns.

La storia weighs heavily upon the narrator's consciousness. But this thing called *la storia* is at best problematic because it can only be engaged through the troublesome and imprecise medium of language. Whatever the facts, whether an ornate marble sarcophagus or an historical incident, they must be defined by words. The narrator tells us that "Words are perhaps border conditions between speakers and objects . . . Words are aromas," which suggest or intimate but seldom fix reality. Even more troublesome, he says of those Italian immigrants who settled his neighborhood that "L'Astoria wove its fabric of those who could not speak the English or speaking it deploy its references as instruments." Whether of the "ordinary stories of ordinary life lived" in his family or of the great migration or revolutions, *La storia* will always be a tapestry woven on the subjective loom of language.

In *Astoria* it is nearly always the "small distinctions" of "ordinary life" that lead to that Stendhal Syndrome. Sentences often run for pages in an effort to weave the broader patterns of the historical tapestry that the narrative voice is trying to understand. These sentences leave the reader breathless and somewhat dazed. At other times the narrator tells the intimate details of his Italian family and personal life, mundane and ordinary.

The challenge for Viscusi is that as an Italian American he faces overwhelming problems. He writes in English, when the original tongue of the great historical migration was not even Italian, but now forgotten dialects of Italian. Worse, as if the struggle with language is not enough, Italians know, too, that they are bound by a code of silence, *omertà*. Relatives chastise the narrative voice, "Why tell these things to strangers? Traitor." Ironically, the very act of writing is a betrayal of the narrative Viscusi is trying to write.

For the narrator the French Revolution and the Risorgimento were a revolt against silence. He says that the Risorgimento allowed Italians "to lumber into the twentieth century with all our contradictions squirming together like lizards in a sack." He refers to the "big *we*," which includes those "we" left behind: those Italians who endured the unimaginable carnage of two wars, poverty, and leaders who defy parody in their pomposity and monumental stupidity. For those of us who left, because "we" realized that both Christ and the Risorgimento stopped at Eboli, "we" prospered. Our collective tongues were loosened – we worked, wrote, raised families – and the long historical silence imposed upon the southern Italian *contadini* was broken. Italy's failures were our wound; the Risorgimento was our bow.

Astoria is about history and language, but it is not just a history of Italian immigration. Astoria/*la storia* is multifaceted. Astoria is an honest reach for the meaning of the great migration, the meaning which continues to change with each new generation. L'Astoria/*la storia* keeps shifting under our feet. The narrator tells us that Astoria is no longer an Italian immigrant neighborhood. Perhaps now it is a Greek neighborhood or Puerto Rican, or it is filled with professors or doctors who speak correct English. But it doesn't really matter. It remains where it had always been from the beginning: "*la storia* as it becomes what keeps writing itself under what you write or hear, a dialect inaudible, invisible, and if heard then only as auroras around something inescapably lucid and vividly wrong, but nothing more palpable than the sign that even under the nymphs at the Opéra, you weren't there." But "we" all know that "we" were in L'Astoria, once, and still are.

Women as Lovers
by Theresa Carilli

Theresa Carilli has a Ph.D. from Southern Illinois University and is currently Associate Professor of Communications at Purdue University. Her plays have been produced in California and Australia. *Women as Lovers* contains two short plays, "Dolores Street" and "Wine Country," both set in the northern California lesbian community.

Carilli's plays must be read in the cultural/political context in which they appear. Her job is a difficult one. On the one hand, her goal as a playwright is no different from any writer's: she must develop characters who are interesting and believable. But Carilli's task is made more difficult because the current political mainstream in America is not receptive to her lesbian themes and characters. Worse, a certain element of our society even opposes strongly her fundamental responsibility as an artist: to humanize her characters and bring a sense of high seriousness to their lives and relationships.

Carilli succeeds in creating characters and circumstances in her two plays that are both interesting and credible. These are not plays about victimization, but about the lives of women who are struggling with both the political and personal circumstances that fate has handed them. Her major strength as a playwright is the wit and a sense of humor that she brings to her women's tangled emotional lives. Her characters' often critical and satirical view of their San Francisco subculture saves them from any potential melodrama or self-pity. Her characters appear as fallible individuals struggling with very human emotions.

Dolores Street is set in San Francisco and focuses on the lives of four roommates: Lonnie – mid-twenties; Danielle – late thirties; Fran – late thirties; and the youngest in the group, Wendy – late teens. Each woman is allowed a monologue in the course of the two-act play in which she reveals in detail important aspects of her personality. While Carilli's portraits of her characters are candid, they are also sympathetic. Lonnie tells us that now that she is in San Francisco she no longer feels that she is a stranger in America. But she adds sardonically that San Francisco is America's "gay amusement park." In moments like this, Carilli injects wit and humor into her play that balance her characters' serious emotional concerns. They never fall face down into their problems, but always step back and see themselves from a distance.

All four women in the story are, as Lonnie explains, in "process." With such jargon Carilli is both satirizing and dramatizing her characters' struggle to define themselves. Language carries with it cultural and political baggage. Their dilemma is that their received vocabulary is no longer adequate to describe who they are. Each is attempting in some way to find peace of mind in lesbian culture. Fran, for example, was once married and now must define for herself another kind of life. However their individual pasts might distinguish them, all the women are seeking a long-term, committed relationship.

When the play opens, they are all sitting at a table reading personal ads in the newspaper. Fran is contemplating writing one to find an acceptable partner. Lonnie and Danielle have recently been jilted and have to deal with feelings of betrayal and loneliness. As they read through the ads, Carilli satirizes the San Francisco subcultures that surface through the fissures that anonymous personal ads offer, from witches and astrologers to anti-smoking vegetarians. Their plan is to have a dinner and to invite those who respond to their ad. The humor and irony is that poor Fran is merely looking for a well-balanced woman who will share her sense of commitment. Where she might find that person among the bizarre, crackpot ads is anyone's guess.

When the fateful night arrives, the dinner party is a bust. We are never allowed to see the wild assortment of guests. As they congregate in the kitchen, the four women tell us that their dinner guests off stage include a nurse, a carpenter, a computer nerd, an accountant who wears flowered bellbottoms, a "cosmic momma" with sparkles on her ears, and a writer of women's erotica. Upon entering the kitchen, Wendy exclaims, "Bizzaro." Fran says, "They're not my type."

In contrast to their unsettled lives, the women observe every day on the balcony next door a couple that is refinishing a piece of furniture. The couple becomes for the women an example of that commitment and domesticity that they are all seeking and that San Francisco subculture cannot offer them. In the closing scene, Wendy tells Lonnie – referring to their neighbors – "I want a relationship just like theirs, at least a relationship that looks happy."

In *Wine Country* Carilli takes greater risks. Her *dramatis personae* include five women: Jo, Robin, Jamie, Margaret, and Sally. These women share intense love relationships. But Carilli's critical view of her characters' behavior does not allow her one act play to descend into melodrama. Robin, a professional photographer, exploits people for her professional and emotional needs. Jamie, her model, is equally self-centered in her relationships. In the outcome of the tangled plot, Carilli does not allow any of her characters the luxury of playing the victimized partner. They all have a capacity for lies and deception. In the end, Carilli returns again to the theme of commitment. Jo asks Sally, "Are all relationships just temporary?" Sally, who has jettisoned Margaret for Jo, responds callously, "All relationships."

However our current political mainstream might wish to define the contents of *Women as Lovers*, Carilli has created characters who transcend their local circumstances. Her women are dealing with the fundamental and universal theme of commitment that is ultimately a concern for all classes and genders. At the same time, Carilli's characters labor under a different kind of pressure as lesbians in American society. As Jo says, "Ask yourself what it feels like to have to tell the world that you are single, even if you have been living with the love of your life for years. Ask yourself how you're gonna tell your family members. Ask yourself how it feels not to be included as a couple by relatives." But Carilli makes it clear that such pressures do not excuse her characters from taking personal responsibility for their behavior. Carilli holds the mirror up, which has always taken courage in any culture, especially for an Italian American woman.

Paper Fish
by Tina De Rosa

Paper Fish was originally published in 1980 by a small press and immediately dropped from sight, not an uncommon beginning for most Italian American novels before 1980. Its author, Tina De Rosa, grew up in Chicago, Illinois. From 1977 to 1982 she was a writer in residence at the Ragdale Foundation in Illinois, where she completed *Paper Fish*, which won the manuscript-in-progress award from the Illinois Arts Council. In 1981 it was nominated for the Carl Sandburg Award. De Rosa has published short stories and has completed a second novel.

Paper Fish focuses on three generations of the BellaCasa family and is set in Chicago's westside Italian neighborhood, demolished decades ago. Since World War II, it has been the fate of such ethnic enclaves to become the site of urban redevelopment projects. No doubt De Rosa created *Paper Fish* out of the pain of the obliteration of her community and that sense of irretrievable loss. The novel is a recollection that covers the years from 1949 to 1958. But this is not a sentimental memoir. Instead, it is a cleverly written story driven by a powerful undertow of emotion in every section of the non-chronological narrative.

While the form of De Rosa's novel is innovative, its content is derived from those familiar elements of what I will term the classic Italian American narrative tradition. This is not an immigrant narrative like *Christ in Concrete* about the initial struggle of the first generation to establish itself in North America. Rather, this is the story of the second generation's attempt to define its identity and its place in American society. *La Storia* (history), which is expressed through the images of Italian folk culture in the story, is central to De Rosa's narrative.

The story begins with the Prelude, a page and a half prose poem that begins, "This is my mother, washing strawberries, at a sink yellowed by all foods, all liquids, yellowed. This is my mother scalping the green hair of strawberries . . ." It is not fortuitous that De Rosa begins her story with an image of her mother. In *Paper Fish* women are the arbiters and conduits of family history, tradition, and values. The narrative is about the BellaCasa family: Marco, Sarah, their daughters, Doriana and Carmolina, and Marco's aged mother, Grandmother Doria. The BellaCasas make up a typical working-class, three-generation Italian American family. Marco, the young father, is a policeman. His immigrant mother, Grandmother Doria, lives across the alley. Sarah is Marco's second-generation Lithuanian wife.

Though happy and secure, the members of the BellaCasa family must face a dilemma which threatens not only its values but its very identity. From birth, Doriana, the first born, is locked in her own private world from which she is unable to communicate with anyone. As her grandmother describers her, she got "lost in the forest," never able to participate fully in family and community life. What to do with her becomes the major question in the story that plagues Marco, Sarah, and Grandmother Doria.

The prospect that Doriana might be sent away to a clinic pro-foundly affects her younger sister, Carmolina. Doriana's poten-tial abandonment becomes a theme throughout the narrative that challenges the core of the Italian family's identity and values.

Surrounding the sometimes troubled BellaCasa family are the people that composed all immigrant neighborhoods known as Little Italies in America at the time. The characters that De Rosa describes have become archetypes in this classic form of the Italian American narrative. There is Schiavone the butcher, Stephanzo the fish man, Giovanni the watermelon man, Tony the barber, La Scala the baker, Augie the grocer, and Gustavo the vegetable man, whose blind horse pulls his wagon. One evening from his stoop Marco observes as "The peanut vendor passes by, the slow smell was of peanuts in the air . . . in the vendor's bright green wagon. Down the street, the watermelon stand shone like a white jewel in the night. The slices of watermelon rested on fine shavings of ice like dia-monds . . ." De Rosa is able with such characters and images to evoke not just the neighborhood atmosphere but a way of life.

Part of any Italian immigrant community at the time was the obligatory band of gypsies, who were as much a part of the folklore and myth of Italian culture as they were a physical presence. In the BellaCasa neighborhood they unexpectedly move into a storefront. De Rosa describes them, with their "golden jewelry and . . . silver combs in their hair," as "terrify-ing" and "beautiful." In the folklore of their Italian neighbors, they are mythological figures. They ride black horses that were once devils. When they go by a house, they can turn goats' milk sour and chickens can become barren. Whenever gypsies pass Italians on the street, they make a hasty sign of the cross to protect themselves against *malocchio.* All the neighbors live in fear that the gypsies might kidnap their children. They are the maligned "other" in this ethnic community.

Like the folktales about the gypsies, De Rosa's narrative dramatizes the folk rituals that organize her characters' daily lives and define them as people. Throughout, De Rosa gives us fragments of memory that recall Grandmother Doria's wedding feast in Italy and intimate details of Marco and Sarah's wedding night. When Marco dies, at her husband's funeral the widowed Sarah reflects upon her life with Marco: the great flow of ritual events over more than twenty years, beginning with their wedding, the births of their children, their family life, and now his funeral. Such memory fragments serve as signs that not only define De Rosa's characters but define the history and meaning of the Italian American experience.

Grandmother Doria is the family matriarch, and it is through her that all tradition must pass. Widowed years before, she lives across the alley where Marco and Sarah can always observe her in her daily ritual of washing, cleaning, gardening, and cooking. In her busy life, images of Italian folkways abound. In the summers, she can always be seen hanging red peppers on her clothesline between the sheets, which take on the fresh aroma of the peppers. She organizes the obligatory outings to Grandfather BellaCasa's grave. With a picnic basket stuffed with bread, onions, tomatoes, and wine, the BellaCasa family, including an assortment of aunts and uncles, spends the afternoon at the grave site picnicking and planting flowers while the children play.

One day in her old age, she realizes that she will never live to see Carmolina married. So out of respect for her grandmother, Carmolina dons a wedding dress and in a ritual procession the neighborhood men carry the ailing Doria to her granddaughter's room. There they share a poignant moment together in which the maternal tradition of the BellaCasa family is transferred to the twenty-one year old Carmolina, who must assume the responsibility of carrying the family culture forward to a new but uncertain future.

The novel ends with an Epilogue of six, short, fast-paced fragments. The neighborhood is destined to be destroyed by "progress." Giovanni the watermelon man yells at Stephanzo the fish man, "Where you go," as he and his wife pack the furniture, family pictures, and children into their truck. As De Rosa concludes, "Berrywood Street had disappeared as though it were a picture someone wiped away." Not quite. In its innovative form, but classic images, *Paper Fish* is Berrywood Street's dramatic and passionate resurrection. *La Storia* remains a powerful theme in the Italian American narrative, which, it seems, will not remain silent until all such neighborhoods are resurrected.

Native Italian Writers in North America

The Rain Came Last and Other Stories
by Niccolò Tucci

The Rain Came Last and Other Stories is the first English translation of Tucci's short fiction. His stories focus on the tangible and familiar: family and society. His realistic style evokes a strong sense of place and time. He renders well the conditions of the Italian *borghese* as well as the difficulties of the vulnerable northern Italian peasantry. When Tucci is not dramatizing the high seriousness of his characters' struggle for survival, he captures with great humor the foibles of Italians when they are confronted with their bureaucratic institutions. Tucci's Italy is divided by class and run by a bureaucratic government. Yet his Italy survives only because the family serves as a stronghold against social chaos.

Tucci is a product of the bicultural and transatlantic experience of this century. He was born in Switzerland in 1908 before moving to New York City. His father was an Italian and his mother a Russian. He writes that he is "by nationality a planetarian." His stories cover his childhood in Tuscany and adult life in New York City. Tucci writes in the first person, out of politeness, he says, to his readers. This gives his stories an immediacy and an autobiographical tone.

In "Terror and Grief," the first story in the volume, he writes of his brothers' and sisters' fear each time that his parents leave them with their governesses and tutors for an extended holiday abroad. This is a story of how, amidst all of the petty conflicts that are a part of childhood, the children in the story managed to pull together in their common bond of their love of their parents and their unspoken anxiety over the void that their parents created with their periodic absences. To avoid confronting their collective "derelict conditions," they immerse themselves in reading and their study of languages. At times their suppressed anxiety flares into open conflict. But in the end they make a ritual confession and reaffirm their sibling bond.

Whatever the conflicts among his characters, the family ultimately is the anchor that stabilizes their lives. In the "Beautiful Blue Horse," a story filled with subtle irony and understated humor, the family disagrees over the value of Nello, a Hungarian horse that the father purchases. Nello is a foreigner, like their Russian mother. The value and use of the horse is problematic, until they all find "a common ground of understanding, to work together for the good of the family." Besides, after seven years, the father sells Nello to buy the family car. The horse evokes a sense of history and with its passing comes change within the family. When the horse is gone and it is replaced by the new car, the family remains, nevertheless, stable and secure.

In "History Comes C.O.D.," Tucci explores class warfare, Italian style. Count Geppo Quaderni refuses to believe that the administrator of his estate, Bartoli, is stealing from him. He blindly ignores the old Tuscan proverb, *"Chi dice fattore dice ladro"* (Who says administrator says thief). The history of the upper-class' exploitation of the peasantry is repaid. He loses everything to the cruel Bartoli family and is allowed to be buried on the estate because his grave will only add value to the property.

In "The Siege," Tucci and his family wait for the arrival of Vladimir, the mother's oldest son from a previous marriage, who went off to war. Three years later they receive a letter from him that informs them that he is coming home, but not when. His return becomes the family's dream and the mother's obsession. She waits each day at the window and shuts out "the loudest expression of reality" that surrounds her in the house.

Waiting for the prodigal son becomes "a family epidemic, a strange fever." For Tucci, the family is more than an association of people: it is a living organism that can become ill and can collectively degenerate if one member becomes distraught. In Tucci's family all must endure pain even when one member is afflicted. The family waits in vain for the return of Vladimir.

In "The Rain Came Last," Elia, a peasant, is killed in a hit-and-run accident. The convertible, occupied by upper-class people wearing "veils, scarfs, sunglasses, [and] tennis caps," races away. Its occupants and driver are indifferent to Elia's plight. The peasants' fate is likened to the unpredictable and indifferent elements that lash across their forbidding landscape. The social order is no less indifferent. Not only does the car speed off, when the doctor and brigadier arrive at the scene of the accident, they are impatient to get home out of the inclement weather and hurriedly write the accident report. Only the peasant's wife, pregnant and now widowed with seven children, is left to mourn.

Tucci lightens his tone and parodies the stupidity of Benito Mussolini's efforts to militarize Italian society in "The Military Intelligence." One day Il Duce decrees that a course and examination in "military culture" must be required of all university students. To subvert the edict, professors suddenly cultivate interests in such obscure fields as Sardinian folklore and revert to long lectures on ancient Greece. When they do finally teach Italian history, their lessons turn into pointless debates over the minutia of military battles. In the end the narrator faces his examiners in an oral examination without knowing any answers to the questions. But due to an ambitious colonel who must secure his advancement in the military bureaucracy, he declares all of the narrator's answers correct. No one on the committee dares contradict him for fear of his own career. Mussolini's reign finds its appropriate expression in the colonel's absurd revision of history.

The other stories in the volume represent the same subtle craft that characterizes Tucci's style. He captures the historic rigidity of Italy's class society. He illuminates, as well, the human condition, in its folly and strengths. When it goes badly for his characters, we wonder how they can be so blind. When it goes well, we can smile at the methods his Italian characters use to survive. As Tucci says in the postscript to the collection, at an early age he learned from his mother that "the world is a grand place, but baffling. Very baffling indeed." His stories capture not just his sense of confusion but his sense of wonderment as well over the resourcefulness of the individual and the resilience of the family.

Benedetta in Guysterland
by Giose Rimanelli

Giose Rimanelli was born in Italy in 1926. Before he immigrated to the United States in 1960, he gained an international reputation with several novels, all of which were written in Italian and translated into many languages. He has taught at a number of American universities. He is Professor Emeritus at the State University of New York at Albany.

In his introduction to the work, Fred Gardaphé tells us that *Benedetta* was actually written in 1970, more than twenty years before its publication. It was written at a time when the traditional form of prose fiction was being challenged by a select few postmodern American and European writers, such as Italo Calvino in Italy and Robert Coover and Donald Barthelme in America. Like its postmodern counterparts, *Benedetta* is a "liquid" novel without clearly defined boundaries: its plot is convoluted and its theme is obscure. Interestingly, the text of the novel is followed by responses from many of Rimanelli's friends and acquaintances to whom he supposedly sent the novel before it was published. Regardless of who actually wrote the letters, they are a useful addendum to the novel. The letters serve to underscore the point that fiction remains incomplete without its readers' contribution to the imaginative process. The interpretations of the novel remain as limitless as its potential readership.

What we can say for sure about the novel is that it is a story that focuses on Benedetta and her love for Joe Adonis, immigrant and mobster of leisure. But this is not a conventional gangster story. Rather, Rimanelli cleverly parodies the gangster story. Rimanelli's narrative is a torrent of puns, allusions, and made up words. It is more a word puzzle than it is a story about the mafia. Guysterland is a play on gangster. "Days ago" plays on dago. He parodies Italian mobsters' names in such characters as Zip the Thunder and Dio the Boss and even pokes fun at writer Gay Talese in Guy Maltese, a famous "guyster" biographer. Joe runs an olive oil import business, Mamma Mia Importing Co., as a cover for his illicit activities. In guysterland "Guy families deal with each other in guy business." Those who squeal get "kissed." All of the mobsters are from "Paliermu." Appropriately, the novel contains an abundance of gratuitous sex and violence. Benedetta is a nymphet in her youth and devoted, as much as her nature will allow, to Joe in her adulthood. In the end, Joe dies from natural causes in Milan. Benedetta is left forlorn and pregnant with Joe's child.

Yet *Benedetta in Guysterland* is more than a parody of the mafia, which has been done before in a work such as *Prizzi's Honor*. It is an important novel because it challenges the traditional realistic form of the North American Italian novel with its focus on character, social class, and history. Italian American writing is, at its very best, historical and, at its worst, merely the dry bones of a sentimentalized and unusable past. *Benedetta in Guysterland*'s significance is that it discards the realistic model and suggests new possibilities for the North American Italian writer based upon other types of experiences. As a post-World War II Italian immigrant and intellectual, Rimanelli was not a part of the Great Migration at the turn of the century which brought rural, impoverished peasants to North America. Rather, he brought to America another kind of Italian culture – urban, middle class, and educated. His novel reflects what Pasquale Verdicchio has called elsewhere "post-nationalism," that bridging of national boundaries both geographically, economically, and linguistically.

Even more important, *Benedetta in Guysterland* implies, too, that there is a greater diversity in the North American Italian experience and tradition. Just as a new model is needed to replace the stale urban, blue-collar image of Italian immigration, a new criticism is needed to address works such as Rimanelli's. Implicit in the new work is the need for a new definition of what constitutes the Italian American experience and its fiction, a definition that goes beyond the social realism of the North American Italian narrative. Rimanelli's innovative form serves both as a reflection of his social class and as a criticism of the Italian American immigrant experience and culture. It is no accident that the one subject that he would choose to parody in America as an Italian immigrant is the mafia. He parodies not only the sex, violence, and greed that Americans in general crave in their gangster stories, but the very narrative that for too many decades has defined the Italian American identity. As a result, his book reflects the growing diversity within the North American Italian tradition that is already beginning to redefine old models and to redefine the direction of the North American Italian tradition.

Run to the Waterfall
by Arturo Vivante

No matter where Vivante focuses his stories – on a piece of furniture, the Italian landscape, or the inner scape of his characters – he writes with a rare clarity and insight. In addition to its brilliant descriptive passages, *Run to the Waterfall* is also about Vivante's immigration to America. We find in these stories of remembrance both the emotional price of immigration and the psychic dividends it has paid him. Set around the time of World War II, the fifteen stories in the volume challenge the distinction between autobiography and fiction. Deeply emotional, these stories locate an Italy in the writer's mind and heart. It is a place at times of betrayal and at times a place of succor and life-giving sustenance for Vivante as writer and family man. As Jews, Vivante's family fled to England in 1938 just ahead of the Italian fascist persecutions. His family returned to Italy after the war when Vivante then immigrated to America. Like many Italian immigrants, more of the self is left behind than is transported to the diaspora of North America.

Upon his arrival in the United States, he settled in Massachusetts. Since the late 1950s, he has written for numerous journals, including *The New Yorker*. For more than four decades he has been a prolific writer who has not had the notice he deserves. His two early novels, *Goodly Babe* and *Doctor Giovanni*, were well received. Currently, he has more than twenty-one titles in Italian and English to his name.

The stories in *Run to the Waterfall* focus on three members of his family and are set in Siena at the old family estate. The history that Vivante recounts in his stories, unlike the Italian neorealism of the post-war period, is not concerned with the bigger realities of war or social class. Rather, his stories are about his family's past in northern Italy.

There is an undercurrent of sadness that pervades the volume. The history that Vivante writes is actually about the material decline of his once prosperous family. His grandfather was a lawyer and teacher at the University of Rome where his books were required reading for Italian law students. Vivante's father, a philosopher, never achieved the fame of his father. Nevertheless, he dedicated his entire life to his philosophical writing, which was seldom understood by either his family or even his colleagues. The stories that center on his father are touching and sensitively done. He is a character whose mental powers are still strong. Yet, like the fortunes of his family, they are in progressive decline. As the patriarch of the family, he has a profound influence upon his wife and children. He is both revered and scorned by them.

In the story entitled "The Soft Core," Giacomo (Vivante?), the artist son of the family, makes one last effort to reconcile his differences with his aging father. After all, he reasons, his father is old and much of what the family has is because of him. In 1938 as the war approached, he had the foresight to take his family to England before Mussolini began his campaign against Italian Jews. As his father says in another story, "One shouldn't live in a country . . . where one didn't have equal rights."

In "The Soft Core," Giacomo tells us that, in spite of his best intentions, there are those times when his father only infuriates him. Giacomo explains that there are instances when the father asks him for advice on an article only to disregard it as soon as Giacomo offers his suggestions. Even so, Giacomo knows that there is a tenderness behind the tough veneer of his father's character. He is capable of charming the estate's boarders, tourists who stay at the family home each summer. Once, as his father is regaining his strength from a mysterious attack, Giacomo assists him during his rehabilitation. In his weakened condition he laughs and chats amiably with his son. But as he watches his father slowly regain his memory and strength, Giacomo realizes that he can know his father only as "he had been and somewhere . . . still was." He would never change.

No less important to the family's history is the mother. She is a China doll, delicate and fragile. She is a conversationalist who spellbinds her audience with vignettes about the lives of simple people, the political intrigues of popes, or scandals of high officials. She is also an artist who too often relies upon her husband's opinion of her work. Her marriage to her philosopher husband, as Vivante describes it, is "affectionate, loving even, but not passionate, not voluptuous." In "Of Love and Friendship," the mother begins a life-long friendship with a young man named Millo, a poet and collector of rare lichens. They are kindred spirits. Over the years when they are not together, they always manage to correspond. The mother puts as much into her letters to her friend as she does her paintings. When she dies, Millo publishes a selection of her letters which he carefully edits. For thirty years her philosopher husband never appeared jealous of his wife's friend. But now his suspicions are aroused and he broods over what Millo had edited out of the innocent letters.

There are other stories in the volume that treat aspects of the family history in Siena. "The Orchard" centers upon the father's failed efforts to turn the fortunes of the family around by planting a peach orchard and making the estate productive again. But the philosopher father was never known for his business acumen. In "The Chest," Vivante tells the story of a once trusted bailiff for the family estate who had been stealing from the family's storehouse for years. Like Count Quaderni in Tucci's story, "History Comes C.O.D.," the father refuses to believe that his bailiff is stealing and does not heed the Tuscan saying, "*Chi dice fattore dice ladro.*" In "A Place in Italy," with his young family Vivante buys a small farm house near the town of Viterbo in an effort to maintain his connection with Italy and his family's history.

Vivante's stories express yet another aspect of the bicultural experience in North America. His stories span two worlds: they are located in Italian life and culture, but they are written in English. *Run to the Waterfall* is written with sensitivity and insight and displays the hand of a writer who is in command of his craft.

Italian Canadian Writers

The Lion's Mouth
by Caterina Edwards

Caterina Edwards is the product of two (actually three) cultures. She was born in England but grew up in Alberta. Her father was English and her mother was Italian. *The Lion's Mouth*, Edwards' first novel, is a probing and unsentimental look at her bicultural heritage. It is a story about Bianca, an Italian Canadian woman, who ruminates over the life of her cousin, Marco, who lives in Venice. Told in the first person by Bianca, the story shifts between Bianca's quest for her own identity and her concern for Marco and his disintegrating life as husband and father.

Like Edwards, Bianca straddles two worlds: the Italy of her childhood and the Canada of her adult life. Throughout the novel, she unsuccessfully attempts to reconcile the two. In her struggle to come to terms with her Italian past and her Canadian identity, she questions, "Old masks replaced by the new? The vision of the outsider, Italian, American, or Eastern Canadian, superceded by that of the native?" At the same time, her Italian past remains a part of her consciousness. Her Venetian past returns in flashbacks, usually at inopportune and unexpected times. The sudden remembrances "dazzle" Bianca, but they remain only frozen memory fragments on the fringes of her consciousness.

Her past contrasts with her contemporary young adult life of the 1960s and after. Her experimentation as a young woman with drugs, free sex, and radical politics has distanced her

consciousness from the moorings of her Italian past. Her engage-
ment to Jack, a Ukrainian Canadian, and association with his
friends serve only to assimilate her further into Canadian life.

Her cousin Marco becomes for Bianca a representation of
her lost Italian childhood. He is her genetic connection to a dimly
remembered past that continues to bifurcate her identity as a
woman. Marco is surrounded by the splendor of Venetian culture, from its overstuffed museums to its magnificent palaces.
But, as Bianca never ceases to point out, it is also a city in decay.
Venice is sinking into the lagoon. The high tides cover its piazzas
and cobblestoned streets and cause irreversible damage to the
city's treasured art works. Bianca's concern over the loss of such
great works of art is reflected in her concern over the loss of her
past.

Venice's decay also mirrors Marco's personal decline. Bianca agonizes over her cousin's problems: his divorce, a handicapped child, and his psychic disintegration. Bianca's quest for
an understanding of her cousin is a quest for her own identity.
Marco's decline, like Venice's deterioration around him, represents for Bianca the impossibility of reconciling her dual consciousness. As Marco's handicapped child illustrates, not even
genetics can be relied upon. She may be linked to Marco and Italy
culturally and genetically, but her consciousness is also Canadian, an identity she does not reject but cannot totally embrace.

There is no solution to her dilemma. In the end she acknowledges that the "possibility exists," but only the possibility, for
her total acceptance of her life as a Canadian. She admits that she
writes to "exorcise my dream of Venice . . . to rid myself of the
ache of longing . . ." Yet in the end she realizes that she cannot
overcome the spiritual and emotional division caused by immigration and biculturalism. In Marco she seeks "Man below the
masks, below the skin, undifferentiated flesh." She seeks the
same for herself, the Bianca behind the mask. In the end she must
admit to Marco, and to herself as well, "I will never touch you at
all."

Edwards' writing is evocative. She paints a convincing portrait of her characters, especially of her heroine, Bianca, and the dilemma she faces as a Canadian Italian. With terse lines, especially in her dialogue, Edwards brings her people alive.

Vinnie and Me
by Fiorella De Luca Calce

Thirty-three year old Fiorella De Luca Calce was born in Caserta, Italy. When she was four years old, Calce and her family immigrated to Montreal, where she still resides. Calce's first novel, *Toni* (1990) – published in English and later French – was well received in both England and France. *Toni*'s publication history underscores the political and cultural dilemma for Italians in Canada. Official Canadian culture can only be located in *le lingue di inglese e francese*.

Vinnie and Me is yet another successful work for Calce. It is a sensitive treatment of the relationship between teenagers Vinnie Andretti and Piera D'Angelo during their senior year of high school and their last summer together. To the complexity of Quebec's multi-ethnic society in her story, Calce adds the dimension of class. Vinnie and Perri, as her friends call her, are both Italo-Quebecois. Their Italian heritage serves as the basis for their close relationship. Both Perri's and Vinnie's families inhabit that economically insecure working-class strata where first- and second-generation immigrants begin their struggle up the social ladder in Canadian society. Vinnie lives closer to the lower economic rung of society than does Perri. He has an absentee father who left before he was born. His mother attempts to string her emotional life together with unreliable men, who take dope, steal from her, and use her house as a way station.

As a result, Vinnie is a loose cannon. Among his peers he is known as a "loser" and a "clown." He is undisciplined and seldom studies. With so much in his adolescent life out of his control, he is quick to anger and tends to break things in his frustration. His main interest in life is Perri, with whom he plans to take a trip across Canada in the summer of their graduation. As for college, Vinnie admits that he doesn't have "a hope in hell of getting in."

Perri, however, is known as "Miss Perfect" and "Miss Brain" among her peers. She gets good grades and tutors other students. Her mother is deceased, and her alcoholic father, when he is not too ill, works at an unskilled job. In his alcoholic stupor, he at times flies into a rage and hits Perri and Bennie, her younger brother. Perri knows that practicality demands she should attend a business college – Canadian Pacific – upon graduation, but in her heart she longs to attend the Art Institute and become a painter.

Her greatest dilemma is whether to give up painting to pursue the economically expedient path of a business degree. To make ends meet she, with Vinnie, works at a local McDonald's. For lower middle-class ethnics such as Perri in Canadian society, the arts are perceived as more a luxury than a career. As Perri tells Vinnie one day, "I'm not familiar with many rich artists. You think I will make money selling a couple of paintings on Ste. Catherine Street. My father will retire in a couple of years. The house has to be paid. Someone has to take care of Bennie."

Throughout her novel, Calce renders well a sense of the complex multicultural fabric of Canadian society that surrounds her two well-drawn and sympathetic characters. At school Perri has many admirers, among them Sam Lopez. His father is a CEO and his mother is a teacher. Befitting his upper-class station in life, he wears cashmere sweaters and carefully tailored pants. To Vinnie's great chagrin, one day Sam asks Perri over for dinner at his parents. With the Lopez family, Calce dramatizes the culture war and class conflict that characterize Quebec society. The conflict is not between Hispanics and Italians but between the dominant Quebecois culture and the multiplicity of ethnics that inhabit Quebec soil.

At school Vinnie, Perri, and Sam learn French. At home the working class D'Angelo and Andretti families speak Italian and eat pasta. However, at her table Mrs. Lopez pours imported wines and serves "fancy" entrées and *mille feuilles* for dessert. When Mr. Lopez learns that Perri is a painter, he opines, "It's nice to have a hobby." Over their French *haute cuisine*, Mr. Lopez encourages Perri to take typing: "The office might need some extra help. A good job is hard to find nowadays." Later, Sam does not hesitate to discourage Perri from associating with Vinnie, whom he labels a "loser." Economic success and French culture converge at the apex of Quebec's social order. All others remain on the margins of Francophile, Quebec culture.

As the school term draws to a close, Vinnie's and Perri's adult lives loom ominously before them. As they begin to drift apart, Vinnie complains to Perri, "Now all I hear is Canadian Pacific and Sam." Perri has goals: a summer job and a college degree. She does not have time to travel with Vinnie. When her high school counselor tells her one day that the art school she applied to never received her application, she is disheartened. She gave the application to Vinnie. In his selfishness he sabotaged her and failed to turn the material in. But in the end, Vinnie makes up for his deception. Perri is admitted to art school, and she and Vinnie are reconciled.

Vinnie and Me could be categorized as an adolescent novel. It should certainly have a wide readership among high school and young adults. But Calce's stroke is much broader and more sophisticated. She captures well not only the subtle pressures that adolescents in general are under as they approach adulthood but also the particular cultural and economic issues that currently define life in Quebec for its multi-ethnic population.

Fabrizio's Passion
by Antonio D'Alfonso

As a director, novelist, and poet, D'Alfonso is that unique bicultural blend which critics have identified as Italo-Quebecois. D'Alfonso's heritage is Italian. He grew up speaking Italian and French in French-speaking Quebec, but he received his college education in English. *Fabrizio's Passion* was originally published in French under the title *Avril ou l'anti-passion*, before D'Alfonso translated it into English. As a writer of over a dozen books and as a cinematographer, he has struggled most of his adult life with the culture war in Canada between the French and English factions. As he has explained in other contexts, if writers do not publish in either French or English in Canadian society, they are the subaltern other.

With its multiple narration, *Fabrizio's Passion* eschews the conventional form of the novel in its twenty-five chapters. Yet it renders a clear, unified perspective on the Italo-Quebecois experience. D'Alfonso's characters are engaging and never slip into comfortable stereotypes. At the same time, the themes that D'Alfonso develops in his novel are by no means limited merely to the struggles of ethnic Quebecois. Through the particulars of his own experiences in Quebec, he also addresses indirectly the immigrant experience throughout the world.

The novel focuses on the Notte family, post World War II immigrants to Quebec. The opening sets the appropriate historical backdrop for the family. It begins with Lina Notte's diary, which recounts events in the town of Guglionesi in 1944 during the German occupation and the subsequent allied invasion and liberation of Italy. This is followed by Guido Notte's war-time letters to Lina, his soon-to-be wife. Because of the dire conditions in post-war Italy, Guido and Lina immigrate to Quebec in 1950.

With this opening, D'Alfonso sets the appropriate historical backdrop for his characters. For Italian writing, whether in the diaspora or in Italy, *la storia* plays a significant role in the formation of the narrative and development of character.

Fabrizio's Passion is about doubleness: that division of the ethnic writer's consciousness between two cultures, the minority culture and the dominant society. For ethnic Quebecois, their lives are complicated further – culturally, linguistically, and politically – by still being a part of the dominant, English-speaking Canada. Early in the story the young Fabrizio Notte's conflict is expressed in his father's demand that he must attend an English school. Fabrizio grows up in a three-generation Italian household anchored by his Italian grandparents. Fabrizio speaks Italian. However, his father forces him to go to an English-speaking school in French-speaking Quebec because he opposes the cultural hegemony of the dominant French culture. One evening at the dinner table, Fabrizio tells his parents in French that he hates his mother's "soggy" home-made pasta and demands the store-bought kind. Faced with such impudence by his now worldly son, Guido demands that Fabrizio speak the language "your mother taught you."

This type of cultural conflict characterizes Fabrizio's experiences as a boy and as a young man and artist. He quests for some type of center to his conflicted identity. He throws himself into a sensual relationship with Lea Simon. But his efforts to love and to understand the French- and Hungarian-speaking woman only add to his confusion.

Fabrizio's sister, Lucia, faces a similar fate. She brings home Peter Hebert to meet her parents. His real name is Pierre Hébert, but he cannot speak a word of French. With his name change and denial of his French heritage, Peter attempts to assimilate into the dominant Canadian English sector of society. Fabrizio observes, "In many respects, Peter reminds me of all these immigrants' children born in this country. The *difficulté d'être*, the difficulty of being oneself, accrued from an absence of awareness." In spite of her father's disapproval of Peter, Lucia plans to marry him. Marriage for her is liberation from what she considers her "father's dictatorship." Under the dual pressures of English and French cultures, he attempts to control his children's lives in an effort to make them Italian.

Fabrizio asks himself at one point, "what am I? If Canadian, can I say I'm Italian? If Italian, can I say I'm Canadian? Or is my identity purely North American? . . . What is a country? . . . Or worse, what does the age-old myth known as 'roots' truly imply?" His identity must in some way transcend the political ideologies that have plagued Canada and Quebec.

Fabrizio attempts to answer some of these questions in his effort to make a film based upon Sophocles' *Antigone.* For Fabrizio his film is about love, commitment, and family. It is also about transfiguration and transcendence. Antigone must be truthful to herself and honor her brother's memory by giving him a decent burial, in spite of Creon's threat against anyone who tampers with Polynices' corpse. She must be whole in her commitment, not divided between her personal self interest and what she knows is just and honorable.

This is the same kind of division that plagues Fabrizio: how to honor his commitment to family and how to shape his own identity. The script of his film is intertwined in the concluding chapters with Fabrizio's efforts to come to terms with his life, his city, and family, especially the death of Nonna Notte. He says at one point, "To film Italians? How can I find a way of pulling my people out of the holes they've been digging themselves into and lift them to the light of universality? Perhaps our universality lies in our ghettos. I don't know."

Because of his internal conflict, his film project is always on the brink of disaster. Antigone's great dilemma, facing her uncle's wrath and her ultimate death, reflects Fabrizio's conflicted self. In the closing pages of the novel he says, "Nonna, I was asked to talk about myself. But how can I talk about myself by not talking about you, about our family? With your death, everything dies as well. Life and all its struggle seems suddenly so vain."

D'Alfonso ends his novel on this ambiguous note. But in the final image of the novel Fabrizio has a vision in which he dances with Nonna Notte. It is a dance of both recognition and reconciliation. "Nonna," Fabrizio says to his grandmother, "the evening has just begun." He realizes that the resolution of his conflict will be found in a new concept of the family and history.

Beyond the Ruins

by Marco Micone

Marco Micone, a native of Italy, resides in Montreal. With four plays to his credit, he has become an important voice in the political and ethnic discourse in Quebec and Canadian society. Though French-speaking Quebec seeks independence from Canada, Quebec remains a *mélange* of ethnic groups that defies a centrist definition of Quebec society. Micone's *Beyond the Ruins* is an artful treatment of the problems that beset Quebec's ethnic denizens.

Beyond the Ruins is a play in nineteen scenes set in Montreal in 1972 and in a small Italian village fifteen years later in 1987. Its cast of characters include grandparents Maria and Franco (age fifty-five and seventy), Luigi (twenty-seven and forty-three), his wife Danielle (also twenty-seven and forty-three), and their son Nino (fifteen), who appears only in the 1987 village scenes. (He was not yet born in 1972.)

Micone dramatizes well the cultural and psychological bifurcation that life in Quebec entails for the ethnic Quebecois. Maria and Franco are immigrants to Quebec. However, throughout their years in Quebec, Franco yearns to return to their small village, which by 1987 is abandoned and nearly in ruins. One day in 1972, on the excuse that the roof of their unoccupied house in the village is leaking, Franco convinces

Maria to visit the village for two months. But it is all a ruse: their two month vacation lasts for fifteen years – until 1987.

As Andrew Rolle explains in *The Italian Americans: Troubled Roots,* Maria and Franco represent that conflicted class of immigrants known as *golondrinas,* birds of passage. When they immigrated to Canada, Franco felt that he had become separated from his roots. Then, upon their return to Italy, they became separated from family and friends that they left behind in Quebec. Worse, over the fifteen years that they live in the decaying village, Maria is denied the enjoyment of watching her grandson, Nino, grow up. Yet the churlish Franco is content. At one point he growls, "As long as I'm alive, the village won't die. That will be my revenge for all those who were chased away." He turns the immigrant's resentment toward Italy on its head and returns.

Luigi, like his father, cannot expunge the village from his consciousness. Though born in the village, he lived most of his adult life in Quebec. But he says to his father upon meeting him in the village in 1987, "At least you have a country. You lived here long enough to feel it's home. For me, home is nowhere. My home is neither in Montreal or here in these stones, in these hills. My home is in my head . . . But I always feel there's something or someone missing."

In 1987 he takes Nino to the village to introduce his first born to his native land and village. But Nino, typical of the new generation of native-born Quebecois, has no interest in the crumbling, forlorn village. He cannot understand his father's enthusiasm for a place that was emptied by immigration and decayed by the elements. For years Luigi told Nino romanticized stories about the village. But as they stand in the village piazza next to the fountain, Nino says to his father, "It's so different from what I thought. I can't believe people really lived here."

Luigi exemplifies the depths and the complexity of the division of the ethnic Italian consciousness in Quebec. He marries Danielle Laurendeau-Cormier, an upper-class native Quebecois. But as her French name indicates, she is a product of the double, albeit assimilated, consciousness of the native Quebecois. She and Luigi are initially drawn together by their compatible, idealistic political views. They both become involved in a variety of immigrant causes, from labor unions to multi-ethnic federations. They are dedicated political activists who attempt to bring social justice to working-class immigrants in Quebec. Danielle becomes involved to such a degree that she, in the style of modern couples, takes a job in Quebec City for eight years away from Luigi and Nino, who remain in Montreal. As she says, it was "what so many men were doing, just going home for the weekend."

But Luigi's and Danielle's political ideals are not enough to keep them together. In a foreshadowing of their separation, one day early in their relationship Danielle tells Luigi, "I always forget you're Italian. My parents, my friends, none of them think of you as Italian . . . I don't know why you're so intent on being Italian. You could easily pass for a real Quebecois." In spite of her political activism on behalf of immigrants, she betrays an ignorance of the ethnic consciousness that she purports to understand.

Luigi responds sarcastically, "A *real* Québécois? Tell me how to behave . . . You have to tell me, my love, what does it mean to be a *real Québécois?* What should I do to become one?" He goes on to voice the dilemma that is at the basis of the cultural conflict and psychological bifurcation that plagues ethnic Italians in Quebec. He takes great offense at Danielle's suggestion that to be a real citizen in Quebec he must give up his identity and become something that is alien to his Italian heritage. In his long speech it becomes clear that a real Quebecois is someone who is upper-class, somewhat Frenchified in name, dialect, or accent, and totally oblivious of his or her heritage. Luigi's sarcastic diatribe ends with a joke that reconciles their differences, but only for the short term. In the end, when they visit his decayed southern Italian village, they discover that their interests and lives are irreconcilable. Danielle announces to a shocked and angered Luigi that she is leaving her job, abandoning her political ideals, and assuming control of her father's property maintenance company. Luigi hisses at her, "You've always been able to afford the luxury of your every whim. You were a revolutionary sitting around Daddy's swimming pool . . . And now you'll go back to being what you always were: a selfish opportunist who doesn't give a shit about anyone else." They agree to separate.

Micone's brevity in his play is a great asset. He cuts to the chase, develops interest in character quickly, and moves his action along. The change in setting works well and is an effective way to dramatize the cultural chasm that divides the consciousness of his characters.

The Italian American Autobiography

Reunion in Sicily
by Jerre Mangione

The republication of *Reunion in Sicily* is an important occasion. Like Mangione's first book *Mount Allegro* (1943), *Reunion in Sicily* dropped from sight shortly after its publication in 1950. Mangione said that his third book was a casualty of the Korean War era. Art had to wait in the wings. Perhaps, too, we can add, Italian American art had to wait in the margins.

It might also be argued that *Reunion in Sicily* was simply a book for later generations, one that was bound to endure far beyond its publication date. America and Europe wanted to put the war years behind them, while Mangione's classic work was and still is a stark reminder of those post-war years. It may speak to us out of the past, but it addresses many contemporary Italian and Sicilian problems, including a short but startling view of post-war Naples. The section on Naples compares well with another work, now nearly forgotten, John Horne Burns' *The Gallery*, which Luigi Barzini described as a classic portrait of post-war Naples. Mangione had written about Sicily before in *Mount Allegro*, where he detailed the lives of his extended family in Rochester, New York. In the end of that work, in several chilling and sobering scenes, he travels to prewar Italy and Sicily, at the time in the iron fist of Benito Mussolini.

Reunion in Sicily takes up where *Mount Allegro* left off. He goes directly to the heart of the Sicilian problem in all of its tragic consequences for the island's inhabitants. In *Mount Allegro* he focused on the family and ethnic values of his relatives in Rochester. In *Reunion in Sicily* he examines the social and political values of his relatives and their friends who remained behind during the Great Immigration to America in the first part of the twentieth century. He gives a short, stunning portrait of the effects of the war on Naples, where he lands before he begins his journey south to Sicily. When he arrives in the port, he is greeted by his uncle and family, who have been reduced to subsistence level by the war-ravaged economy of Naples. There is no school for the children, and all seven members of the family live in a one-room "cave-like enclosure." His aunt complains, "It is no longer considered disgraceful to steal. People will even steal from their own relatives."

Most of the work centers on Mangione's relatives in the towns Porto Empedocle, Realmonte, and Agrigento. He discovers that his relatives' lives have been shattered by the war experience, from the bombings to the occupation. Through his relatives, Mangione details the cross-currents of political opinion that divided Sicily among the Monarchists, Communists, Socialists, Fascists, and the countless other political parties that complicated Sicily and Italy's struggle toward a democratic form of government after the war. More important, he also tells a very human story in which he shows how the war affected the personal lives of all Sicilians.

Some of his relatives, such as Nardo in Agrigento, in spite of the debilitating effects of the war, continued to support Mussolini. He longed for the reform and order that the deposed dictator promised Italy. For the older generation, the Monarchist Party still had great appeal. Mangione met three old sisters who were born when there was a king and could not imagine life in an Italy without a ruling monarch. Not surprising, the younger generation sought radical reform. Dante, a young poet and neighbor of his relatives in Agrigento, was a committed antifascist, as were all of his friends. But Mangione learns that after the war they all joined different political parties. Dante was a right-wing socialist, his friend Andrea, a left-wing socialist, and Cinga, a lawyer, was a member of Croce's Liberal Party.

One morning, while touring the city, Mangione copied down some slogans that he found on a wall: "Sicily – the 49th American state; Viva Comunismo; Viva Separatismo; Viva DDT." It seems that Sicilians were not without humor over the political divisions that made a ruling majority an impossibility in their war-torn country. When Mangione tried to discuss politics with his relatives, the discussions were reduced usually to shrieking matches in which no one heard what the other was saying. His cousins' opinions often abounded in contradictions, which only reflected the political confusion that surrounded them.

Mangione spent considerable time talking to Sicilian women of all classes. Without regard to social rank, they all believed that America was a veritable wonderland, the place to which they would all one day escape. Interestingly, their image of America was gleaned from Hollywood movies of the period. Peter Bondanella explains in *Italian Cinema* that over 1,600 Hollywood movies were imported to Italy between 1946 and 1950. Italy had been occupied twice by America: once by the American military and once by Hollywood. For the lower-class women Mangione met, America was an Arcadia to which they could escape from their poverty. For the upper-class women he spoke to, America was a country that would free them from the boredom of provincial village life and from the cruel tyranny of their stern Sicilian fathers.

The occupation of the island only amplified Sicilian women's problems. Many American soldiers promised to marry and send for them once they arrived back in the U.S. But, alas, once home in America the soldiers never so much as wrote a single letter to their disappointed Sicilian lovers. Nevertheless, many blindly remained hopeful that their American lovers would one day return to rescue them from their poverty or the oppression of their fathers, who planned to marry them off to unattractive but wealthy suitors. Even worse, for the unwary and less sophisticated young women, many were left with, in addition to their empty promises, fatherless children to raise. Having disgraced their families, these women were disowned, and many were forced into prostitution to support themselves. They became pariahs, the lepers of their society.

Mangione brings a great deal of understanding to a largely misunderstood people. He writes that "in the course of their long history of poverty, havoc and invasion, Sicilians have become so intimate with tragedy that they can take any disaster in their stride." As in the stories of the great Sicilian writer Luigi Pirandello, Sicilians sense that *il Destino* controls their lives. As Mangione explains, this tragic sense is rooted in ancient Sicilian culture when pagan gods controlled lives and events. Christianity has not altered Sicilians' view of life much, nor has their colonial history helped to change the way they look at themselves or their society.

But, in spite of their diminished expectations, Sicilians do have some hope. Even if they cannot control their fate, they still take pleasure in the moment – what little life might have to offer. As Mangione says, "Essentially the people were at peace with themselves. Their future might be more dreadful than their past. But nothing could deprive them of their oldest and most consistent achievement: a basic harmony between themselves and the experience we call living."

American Dream: An Immigrant's Quest
by Angelo Pellegrini

The North American Italian autobiography is a sometimes duplicitous form. Pellegrini's *American Dream* and Jerre Mangione's *Reunion in Sicily* make a good pair because they expose this duplicity. Pellegrini's work is about the Italian Self in America while Mangione's is about the Self in Italy. Each work contains in a sublimated manner what is absent in the other. Mangione is really writing about and to America, though the Self is in Sicily. By contrast, Pellegrini is writing about and to Italy, though the Self is in the Pacific Northwest. The North American bicultural consciousness cannot escape the contrast between Italy and America. Pellegrini tells of his great success in America. But on another level he is writing home to Italy – which remains an inextricable aspect of his consciousness – to explain why and how he has succeeded in America. Indeed, in *Immigrant's Return* (1951), his first return visit after three decades to his native village, he articulated the same theme when he wrote that the Old World was "a yardstick by which I have been able to take the dimensions of the New World." In *American Dream* he orders the chaos of *la storia* – his former life in Italy.

Mangione, by contrast, goes to visit his relatives in war-torn Italy, in all of its economic, moral, and social chaos, and writes home to that *La Merica* in his mind's eye, that place of social, moral, and economic order. In both works the Self is aloof: it constructs order out of historical chaos, family out of disintegration, and personal success out of the despair that existed in Italy at the time of the Great Immigration and again after World War II. Mangione confronts the fate that would have been his in southern Italy and Sicily if his family had not immigrated, just as Pellegrini celebrates his success and his avoidance of the sad fate that nipped at his and his parents' heels as they immigrated to America in the nick of time.

Angelo Pellegrini arrived in America at the age of ten and settled with his family in McCleary, Grays Harbor County in the state of Washington. In 1913, when he and his family arrived in the Pacific Northwest, the opportunities in his new environment were staggering. This was an immigrant experience that differed radically from the eastern, urban, immigrant life that Oscar Handlin described in *The Uprooted* (1951). Pellegrini recalls that "The land we needed was ours for the asking.

Firewood littered the landscape. There was game in the hills and fish in the waters. The internal organs of beef cattle – liver, heart, kidney, tripe – were given freely to us who were barbarians enough to eat them. Father had a job. Mother, with the aid of the children, took in boarders. We had cows in the barn, pigs in the sty, rabbits in the hutches, chickens in the henhouses. On rich land that had never been cultivated we grew all our vegetables and some of our fruit." Pellegrini writes, "In less than a year after our arrival we were rich." His story reflects Italian immigrant experience in the West that Andrew Rolle documented in *The Immigrant Upraised*, which he wrote as an answer to Handlin's depressing view of urban immigrant life. While immigrants that settled in the East and West shared the same uprootedness and alienation from their collective past, the Italian immigrant in the West simply had more resources and more space to begin the upward struggle in the new land.

But *American Dream* is not just another rags to material riches story. Rather, Pellegrini's parents were more concerned with providing the necessities for a stable family life than with accumulating wealth or climbing the social ladder. His father had opportunities for land investment. But his parents disregarded anything that did not bolster the security of the family.

As result, *American Dream* is a chronicle of Angelo Pellegrini's intellectual and spiritual growth in the Pacific Northwest. As he charts his progress through the public educational system, he describes his acculturation as an Italian immigrant into the new values of the democratic society he adopted. But as he wrote, in a classic statement of the bicultural experience, "I had become completely American without having lost my Italian identity, and my Italian descent was beginning to pay dividends."

Pellegrini had the good fortune to come under the tutelage of enlightened, caring teachers. They pointed out to him the value of his heritage and did not discourage in him a knowledge of Italian culture. Pellegrini writes that his education was a quest for what was fundamentally American in his adopted country. His journey took him through a thorough study of American culture, from grade school to the University of Washington, where he came under the influence of some of the nation's "most liberal minds in philosophy, history, literature, and political science." He undertook, too, a study of American jurisprudence in an effort to understand what constitutes individual rights in American democracy. This he found especially interesting because it contrasted so dramatically with the hierarchical, peasant society he had left behind in Italy. He completed his education with a Ph.D. in literature. He went on to a distinguished career in teaching and writing for nearly thirty years at the University of Washington, where in 1967 he retired as Professor Emeritus of English.

His quest, however, was not without its setbacks. In the midst of the Great Depression he found a society totally at odds with its expressed ideals of equality and freedom. He writes of the wealthy industrialists, "As rugged individualists, they did not hesitate to use government to promote their ends, and as rugged individualists they sought to eliminate competition. They succeeded in doing both." Unemployment was high and wages were low. The depression led to a collapse of fundamental rights, from freedom of speech to freedom of assembly. Disillusioned, he joined the Communist Party in 1934, only to resign a short time later because he discovered that the party's activities were "irrelevant to the challenge posed by the depression."

After the war and during the McCarthy era, his brief membership in the Communist Party came back to haunt him. Pellegrini was called as a witness before the Joint Committee on Un-American activities that was investigating one of his colleagues. As a previous member of the Communist Party, Pellegrini realized that if he were forced to appear, all that he had worked for in his youth would be destroyed. The hastily convened panel was little more than a kangaroo court composed of ambitious political hacks. But luck was on his side. Because of the court's ineptitude, he was never called. The court was disbanded and never reconvened. In what would have been just a few minutes of testimony before that court of Yahoos, Pellegrini's American dream would have turned to ashes.

The 1950s became for Pellegrini a period of unexpected success. The land of opportunity did not withhold its bounty from him. In 1948 he published his first book, *The Unprejudiced Palate*, which brought him immediate national acclaim and launched a writing career that would continue for another four decades. *American Dream* reflects the complexity of the North American bicultural experience. Janus-like, it looks both ways. While on one level it is about success in America, indirectly it is also about failure in Italy – what it refused to do for its fleeing emigrant population. Pellegrini's work is a classic statement of the immigrant's transplantation in the New World and his subsequent success.

Discovery and Definition

North American Italian Women Writers

The Dream Book:
An Anthology of Writing by Italian American Women
edited with an introduction by Helen Barolini

The publication of Helen Barolini's *The Dream Book* is a milestone in Italian American women's writing. *The Dream Book* is a kind of manifesto that informs us that Italian American women are a distinct voice with a unique point of view, separate in many ways from Italian American men. If Italic writing in general has struggled for recognition in Canada and the United States over the last half century, then Italic women writers have carried a double burden.

In her well-written and carefully researched Introduction, Barolini asks why Italian American women haven't achieved the prominence in American writing that they deserve. Her answers are manifold and complex. Basically, she explains that from childhood to adulthood the Italian American woman was required "to put herself under the protection of a man." Though she points to some notable exceptions, Italian culture did not allow women to exercise independence from the family. Often in Italian fiction, female characters are strong, independent types. But the lives of even the strongest female characters are more often than not circumscribed by the time consuming tasks of organizing the family and fighting poverty, especially for immigrant mothers.

Historically, women were not encouraged to pursue formal education. As the all too familiar saying informs us, *"Fesso chi fa il figlio meglio di lui"* (It is a stupid man who makes his son better than he is). This mentality, especially pronounced in southern Italian culture, was applied even more stringently to Italian daughters. This not only denied them marketable skills but, more importantly, it isolated them from other women who shared their concerns and point of view. *The Dream Book* breaches the barrier that has historically separated Italian American women writers from each other and acknowledges them as a distinct group with a special heritage. They are no longer, in Barolini's words, "silent women."

The fifty-six women represented range in age from their twenties and thirties to their eighties. Barolini has divided her collection into five sections: Memoirs, Nonfiction, Fiction, Drama, and Poetry. Even though they write in traditional literary forms, Barolini argues correctly that Italian American women writers are creating new models that are redefining the intellectual and social roles of Italian American women. This is a complex task, as Barolini suggests, because Italian American women must bridge two cultures and, in the process, shatter the delimiting stereotypes that have been assigned to them in both the Italian family and society in general.

The collection includes well-known figures such as novelist Mary Gordon, poet Diane di Prima, and lesser known writers. Included are some intriguing discoveries that only reinforce Barolini's point about the invisibility of Italian American women writing in America. Antonia Pola, pseudonym for Antonietta Pomilla, is among those "lost" writers. She published one re-remarkable novel in 1957 and has never been heard from since and cannot be located. Other writers include Maria Mazziotti Gillan, Lynette Iezzoni, Maryfrances Wagner, Anna Monardo, and Rose Carmellino, who won the UNICO literary award in the 1980s.

Playwright Michele Linfante, recipient of a National Endowment Playwrighting Fellowship in 1981, has the only play in the volume.

Though the writers represent great diversity in class and generation, they are unified by the images of women that they portray and celebrate. They express what it means to be ethnic in a pluralistic society such as ours. In Memoirs, among the seven writers featured, we find images of the immigrant women as self-sacrificing survivors. Rosa Cassettari, who arrived in America in 1884, writes of how she struggled stoically and alone with her children in a foreign land. In her reminiscence, third-generation Italian Mary Gordon tells the poignant story of a great aunt, Zi'Marietta, who gave her life "to beauty," thus relegating her life merely to creating a self that would please men. For this generation of women, their strength and perhaps their tragedy as well, whatever their station in life, was their abnegation of the self.

In the Nonfiction section, Frances Winwar, Barbara Grizzuti Harrison, Carol Bonomo Ahearn, Rosemarie Santini, and Gioia Timpanelli dissect the complexity of the bicultural experience for Italian women in North America. Harrison objects to the passive image of women in Coppola's Godfather films, while Ahearn examines the variety of women in Puzo's *The Fortunate Pilgrim* and Barolini's *Umbertina*. As her title implies, "Definitions of Womanhood: Class, Acculturation, and Feminism," Italic fiction has begun, especially in Barolini's novels, to rescue the Italian American women from their submissive role as the domestic survivor.

The diversity of voices, as well as the options now available for Italian American women, become even more obvious in the Fiction and Poetry sections. The fifty-three writers included address a wide variety of experiences: from Italians in Vermont, New York, Philadelphia, Chicago, to Colorado, San Francisco, and the San Joaquin Valley. Biculturalism and the Italian American experience are integrally linked with the regionalism that has always characterized American literature from its beginnings. In addition to locating Italian ethnicity in particular regions of the country, these stories explore the central role that Italian women play in the Italian family.

Diversity comes in another form in the poetry section. From Diane di Prima to Maria Mazziotti Gillan, the voices that sing in this section challenge stereotypic images of Italian women in North America. Di Prima's odyssey as Beat poet, student of Zen, and feminist is recorded in nearly four decades of her poetry and defies all stereotypes of the Italian American woman of her generation. Her struggle to be heard in a male dominated era and art form is a story in itself. Maria Mazziotti Gillan in "Public School No. 18" writes of her struggle to assimilate as a youngster, until one day, she discovers, "I have found my voice." This is what characterizes all the poets in this section. Each has found her voice. *The Dream Book* is an important step in relocating Italian American women writers from the margins to the center of not only Italian American writing but of American literature.

The Voices We Carry:
Recent Italian/American Women's Fiction
edited by Mary Jo Bona

The Voices We Carry is a collection of fiction written by some of the most distinguished Italian American women writing today. Editor Mary Jo Bona, professor of American literature at SUNY, Stony Brook, has divided her collection into four categories: The Recreation of Historical Lives; The Intersection Between America and L'Italia; La Famiglia in America; and The End of a Generation. Bona's categories are well chosen and represent the major aspects of the Italian American experience, especially since World War II.

One of the most outstanding pieces in the collection is Mary Bush's "Planting." Bush, who teaches creative writing at Cal

State Los Angeles, is a widely published writer and is the winner of the 1985 PEN/Nelson Algren Award. "Planting" is a story about the Italian immigrant, Serafine, and her family as they struggle to survive on a Mississippi Delta cotton plantation at the turn of the century. Bush writes about an aspect of the Italian American experience that has had little notice over the years. As field workers, Serafine and her children endure living conditions that are considerably worse than those they left behind in Italy. The company controls every aspect of their lives. Serafine and her children live on subsistence wages and are denied education. The Italian immigrant's plight is parallel to the condition of African Americans who work on the plantation with them and suffer the same racial prejudice.

In her Viet Nam-era story, "Americans: One Minute to Midnight," Daniela Gioseffi makes a similar connection to other American ethnic groups as her main character, Dorissa, urges her daughter "to discover our roots . . . the way Jews and Blacks are doing." In the "Lost Era of Frank Sinatra," Rachel Guido deVries' lesbian character, Jude, struggles with her isolation from her family. But in the end she draws strength from the generations of Italian women in her past and reaffirms the importance of family and her roots as an Italian American woman.

In the next section, The Intersection Between America and Italy, Lisa Ruffolo's "Southern Italy" recounts the story of Italian Americans and others traveling in Italy. Laura Marello's "Claiming Kin" focuses upon the divorce between an Italian man and an Italian American woman and the difficulties they face in their family's transatlantic separation. In one of the most original stories, "Desert Ruins," set in the American Southwest, Dodici Azpadu writes about the connection between the colonization of Native Americans and the colonization of the indigenous Siculi of Sicily centuries ago by Greeks and North Africans.

It is especially pleasing to see Italian American writers addressing the interconnectedness of the American ethnic experience. I would include deVries' story here as well. Too often the culture war, including the discourse within the gay community, over the last thirty years has erected barriers rather than promoted understanding. These stories suggest grounds for cross-cultural understanding, not territorial divisiveness.

In perhaps the most psychologically probing story of the collection, "Bernie Becomes a Nun," Susan Leonardi dramatizes Bernadette Palermo's emotional decision to leave her family for the convent, which serves as her new family for more than two decades. Adria Bernardi, Phyllis Capello, and Giovanna Capone all treat the centrality of the family in Italian American life in their stories as well.

In the final section of the volume, The End of A Generation, Dorothy Bryant, Anne Paolucci and Lynn Vannucci all address the passing of the first generation of immigrants to America. As we begin the twenty-first century, we realize that those who made the supreme sacrifice to separate from land, home, and kin are passing from our midst. These are mournful stories, but fitting tributes to the courage of those immigrants who came to America at the turn of the last century.

Mary Jo Bona has made a significant contribution to Italian American and women's studies with her collection. She has brought together quality writing that explores what it means to be a woman and an Italian American. She has also written an intelligent and insightful introduction to the collection.

Poetic Voices

NORTH AMERICAN ITALIAN POETRY

A God Hangs Upside Down
by Joseph Maviglia

Joseph Maviglia is a Canadian Italian poet whose relatives emigrated from southern Italy after World War II. He is a member of a generation of Italian Canadians that grew up in post-war North America. Maviglia cogently addresses in his work both the immigrant experience of his forebears and the second generation's efforts to come to terms with its complex heritage.

The first task that Maviglia faces is to find an appropriate voice with which he can express the nature of his bicultural experiences, both his personal experiences as a middle-class Canadian and his immigrant, southern, Italian heritage. Linguistic, cultural, and class divisions separate him as a second-generation Italian from the immigrant and southern Italian experience. Yet he must give voice to his southern Italian forebears who had no voice – economically, politically, or socially – in their own land with their Calabrese dialect. When they arrived in North America, they found that they had no voice again, for all the same reasons, in industrialized, English-speaking Canada. Theirs was not a willful code of silence. Rather, they had neither the language nor the economic power to express their values or to describe their struggle.

From the distance of a generation, Maviglia's task as a poet is twofold. He must bridge the historical and cultural gap that separates him from Italy and the immigrant class. At the same time he must give an authentic voice to those struggling, immigrant peasants who speak in his poems. He succeeds on both fronts. His poetry is distinguished by his clear, direct language. His metaphors that capture the emotional essence of his experiences are exact and without pretense. There is no straining in his language. Rather, there is the feeling of a direct connection between the thing and the word, the experience and the line.

In the opening poem in the volume, "Stone," Maviglia writes about a distant time, "somewhere before centuries" and about his own problematic identity as an individual and poet: "and I / not truly of a shape I recognized." But this was "before the birth of fire" and the birth of his own imagination which lights the way through his problematic past and present.

What follows in his poems is a chronicle of the immigrant experiences of Concetta, Carlo, and a whole host of relatives and friends. They are all linked by their common experience of separation from Calabria and the struggle for survival in Canada. Maviglia's lines are crisp and hard, like the work experiences he describes, and are devoid of any sentimentality. In "Carlo's Dream," Carlo emigrates: "Leaving the shoreline of his birth / he crawled from mute sea-green / tongue new / America." In "New Language," Carlo's bosses speak English: "Its tone, / mixed with the grating of machines, / digging deep in earth where unbuilt highways sleep, / takes the breath of men / who had a language of their own / before it cracked against a deaf Atlantic."

Carlo, like many other immigrant men, came to Canada alone and then sent for his family. In the section The Song a Shovel Makes, Maviglia begins with an epigraph from Pietro di Donato's *Christ in Concrete,* that classic Italian American novel of bricks, mortar, and suffering. In this section Maviglia gives his immigrants their own voice. In "Carlo," Carlo says, "What will they all write / these sons / these daughters who marry / and leave me / here with myself?" He goes on to say, "If I could write / I would have said: / Poetry is a way of making / sure nobody forgets." Similarly, in "Paolo di Pietro" Paolo and his wife lose a son, and he voices his lament in a long soliloquy: "There I am. Each day / another animal. / That is all I am. These / bastards / I build my ass off for."

In other poems Maviglia brings to life the experiences of such men and women as Salvatore, Portuguese John, Remo, Sam, Filippo, Rosetta, and Concetta. The women bear the dual responsibility of childbearing and work in the factories. Maviglia gives his people a place in immigrant and North American history in poems that reflect in their titles the experiences in industrial America: "Job," "Dust and Gravel," "Sweat," "Widower," "Asphalt," and "Sledgehammer."

The history in which they are located is the history of Maviglia's poems. He writes in "Tarantella II," "This tarantella does not / forget its name at Ellis Island or Halifax Harbour / but lives in the hands of field workers / who pass it on to bricklayers / women working in factories / men paving roads / and their children."

But Maviglia's lines are not poetic archeology. Rather, his strong voice in his poems links him to his predecessors in a common endeavor. Fulfilling their longing, he breaks their historical silence. However, as a second-generation Canadian Italian, he must struggle with Italian, specifically Calabrese, as the key to the history of that culture in which he grew up. When he returns to visit Italy, he finds that he faces the same barrier that his ancestors confronted, only now in reverse, with the culture and language of his heritage. In "Brancaleone" he writes that names come to him "in syllables / in a language I've inherited / only part of. / U Calabrisi, Calabrian, I / mangle I've been told. This / has kept me close to silent / since I've arrived."

But in diverse ways throughout *A God Hangs Upside Down* Maviglia breaks his silence and gives life and emotion to his subjects. This is not poetry of victimization or of sentimentality. Maviglia represents in simple language his characters' experiences. You can ask little more of a poet than to see and write clearly. His imagination and poems take flight.

Just West of Now
by Diane Raptosh

Diane Raptosh is a product of a rare form of the bicultural experience. Her experiences in the West and her poems represent an aspect of the North American bicultural experience that has largely been overlooked by scholars and critics. As O. E. Rölvaag's *Giants in the Earth* and Jo Pagano's *Golden Wedding* demonstrate, the Midwest was a destination point for many immigrant groups coming to America at the turn of the century. While there was always a period of "ghettoization" for these immigrants, land was plentiful, from the expanses of the midwestern prairie to California's equally expansive inland valleys and long coast line. Italians and other groups might have settled in communities for a generation or two, but unlike those on the eastern seaboard, ultimately they moved on to higher social ground, and their communities were largely forgotten.

Raptosh is a American of Czech-Italian descent who grew up in Idaho and received her MFA from the University of Michigan. Currently, she teaches writing at the College of Idaho. *Just West of Now* is Raptosh's first book of poems. In clear, precise images, she captures well the Western bicultural experience.

The work is divided into two sections: Place Names and Blood Ties. In the first section Raptosh treats that western and midwestern landscape. In "Transcriptions, Rancho Paradise Motor Park," she writes three dramatic monologues in which she speaks in the voices of her western characters. One is named

Owen, a switchman, who had a debilitating railroad accident and who is relegated to disability. In part II, Max tells of his and his wife's retirement. They wander the great expanses of the western states in an R.V. until the isolation sends them home to a mobile park where they buy "the smallest mobile home there was. / In case we didn't like the town, hitch up, we're on." In part III, Romana, who also lives in a mobile home, speaks of her two husbands and her first memories as a child of "Rock Spring, Wyoming, watching cowboys round up / cattle, chuck wagons and all." She describes the strawberries she planted once, the cows she milked, and the honey they processed from their "Two hundred fifty colonies" of bees. In all three of her dramatic monologues, Raptosh has an ear for the American dialect. Her otherwise controlled lines lengthen as she catches the rhythm and phrases of western American speech in the voices of her working class characters. In their doleful, isolated circumstances, Raptosh's characters are reminiscent of the voices in Edgar Lee Masters' *Spoon River Anthology.*

In the other poems in the sections, she captures well the flavor of her personal experiences growing up in Idaho and her visits to Chicago and Michigan. The poems abound with images from Raptosh's surroundings. Typical of the crispness and clarity of her lines, in "Distance, Weather and Bad Light," a poem to her sister, she recalls "This trek past Shaeffer Butte, we packed / white brick cheddar and the sharpest / possible red." In "Weather Watch," while in Michigan, she receives a letter from Idaho, in which her correspondent reminds her of skiing in winter, foxes and partridges, mountain climbing, and Idaho weather. Still, she writes that in Michigan she is "as much / a part of the landscape here / as a hummock off Lake Superior."

Though Idaho and its images persist in her consciousness, it is a place she has left and has no real desire to revisit. In "Scale," with sharp images of place she ruminates over her brother's return to the homestead in Idaho. In the poem she is attempting to come to terms with her move away from Idaho and home: "Maybe we've both been too long in one place." Likewise, in the title poem to the volume, she writes, "I live convinced, / instead, that memory's the thing to keep / a place intact as is, as was, / or to arrange it as it never was / and never could be, which is what / I'd much prefer."

In the section Blood Ties she explores her Italian-Czech past. "In Black and White of My Mother at Twenty-One," an homage to her mother, she muses over an old photograph: "At this point she knows / she'll marry. Who. / Where. When. She figures time / irons things out. She has / a perfect Roman nose." Her sympathetic portrait of her mother is history that still impinges on the present.

In other poems, she vividly recalls her uncles and aunts and both her Czech and Italian grandmothers. But the landscape in which we find her characters, who often speak in their own voices, is not the typical ethnic urban ghetto, but the ill-defined scape of the western states. In "Emanuela in the New World Garden," Emanuela "finds Arizona, Vegas, Idaho, pretty / much one place, one promise." In the West, Emanuela "is not / found bowing among flora," but instead in the casinos of Las Vegas where she plays blackjack. Yet she still embraces Old World values: "fate. One word / she credits with having coaxed her to this / part of the world."

In other poems, "Concetta's Essay on Poetry" and "Concetta Addresses the Cardinal," Raptosh creates a strong-voiced Italian woman who has her say about poetry and life. In her essay on poetry, Concetta avers that it is life she is after: "Sicily, / the boot. Detroit, A bride. That trinity / of kids. But isn't all this looking / back to try and sculpt time gone / a bit passé?" In her remarks to the cardinal, the aged Concetta confesses to a cardinal her sadness and isolation: "Proud bird, facing passing years, these days / I've found I'm short on pluck." There was a time in her youth when she marked time with Lucky Strike cigarettes she smoked on roof tops in Detroit. Concetta's landscape is barren, with the children gone and little left to fill her days except the birds she keeps as pets. In other poems, "Gloss on Uncle Louie's Finger-nails," "Pullover," "The Guest Bed with Grandma" "Sleeping with Emanuela," and "Mother in the Mountain Pose," Raptosh writes lyrically and sensitively of her Czech and Italian family. In "Sleeping with Emanuela," her Italian grandmother, she writes how the tottering Emanuela "goes to lay her left-/ handed lovely rippled / body down. How at first / it doesn't go. Then it goes."

Raptosh's language is sparse and unpretentious. Absent is the intensity often found in poetry about urban life. Rather, Raptosh's poems reflect the frugal, uncluttered landscape of her western and midwestern experiences. This is the right place for a poet to begin in her first book of poems.

How to Sing to a Dago
by Rachel Guido deVries

How *do* you sing to a dago? DeVries' emphatic answer is with great passion. The thirty-seven poems in her volume are a paean to her family and to physical and spiritual love. This book is a celebration of her Calabrese and Sicilian ancestry, which deVries acknowledges has honed the voice that we hear in her finely wrought poems. The rhythm of her lines is not the casual lilt of conversational poetry, but an aggressive yet lyrical voice that longs to capture "the old ways we danced."

Rachel Guido deVries is the author of a novel, *Tender Warriors* (1986), and one other book of poems. Born in Paterson, New Jersey, she now lives in Syracuse, New York, where she teaches creative writing at Syracuse University. Though she has published only two books of poems, with *How to Sing to a Dago* deVries establishes herself as one of the most important poets to have emerged in the 1990s. She dedicates her book to Diane di Prima, who is something of an oracle for post-war women's poetry.

Her opening poem pays homage to her personal gods – the women in her past who have shaped her character and her voice. In "A Stone, A Ruby, The Sea" she describes her familial predecessors: "I come / from centuries / of Calabrese women / heads hard as stone / I am / shaped by Calabrese women / who breathed near the sea / who are in me / what is in me / What I am." In "Italian Grocer" deVries pays homage to her father who once owned his own store. He caressed his fruits and vegetables as though they were his own children until one day the store burned to the ground. DeVries tells us "Pop went mad and wept / all over the street . . . White / people in the neighborhood said Pop the Wop / torched his own store for insurance. He had none." Here as elsewhere, deVries is never self-pitying or sentimental. In the title poem of the volume, she chants, "Wop wop wop, wop wop a guinea guinea / all day, all day as the dagos on." Despite the denigrating language to Italian Americans, she is able to write, "I mean I can laugh at myself, greaseball." Her strong sense of self absorbs the historical resonances of these slurs and remains resolute in its mission to create.

Even though poets such as Diane di Prima preceded her, as a woman deVries had to struggle to become a writer. Italian culture typically assigned women to domestic roles. In a later poem in the volume, she caricatures her Italian relatives – "Sicilians, Calabrians, / wiseguys and hardheads" – who do not have much respect for her craft or perhaps for her as a woman. A male voice says to her, "Get real. A bird fell outada fuckin' tree. / That's it. So make a big deal of it, / be a poet again . . ." But she has her revenge. She makes finely crafted poems out of their rock-hard heads and foul language. She draws her strength from the women in her life. In "Aunt Jo," she describes her aunt "with a shot of whisky . . . / and a fierce fierce / mouth the one / they say I follow." With the same strength and self-assurance, in the title poem deVries writes, "my voice is like thunder inside of / a storm. I listen to voices that tell me to hush / but I'm hungry for music, in love with all touch."

In the second section of the book entitled "The Notmother Songs," deVries writes passionately about her homosexuality, which complicates her task as an Italian American female writer. *Omertà:* all Italian American writers must face this tribal prohibition against revealing too much about both the self and the family in their works. These poems express the private side of deVries and must have been hewn from even more complex emotions for her as both a lesbian and an Italian American woman. In strong, bold images she celebrates her lesbianism: a "reverence of the body along the lines / of love, the physical planes, my / occasional bliss." In "First Desire / First Time," she writes, "The green of me stretches, lithe, a sapling. I / long for you." In "Ifs for the Notmother from Paterson," she expresses her own dark night of the soul in equally striking images: "I got lost / in limbo I saw like bodiless / heads in blue sky the torsos / of pleasure below where sin lived / and heaven where the rich rose / to the tops of clouds . . ." These passionate poems are resplendent with uncommon images that leap from the page unexpectedly.

In the final section of her book entitled "Birds, Remembering," the spirit of her past is captured in the unifying image of a bird. These poems are the most lyrical and introspective of the volume. They express less a celebration of her heritage than they do "the sorrow and rage" over its passing. In "Birds of Sorrow," she recalls painful images from her family and childhood. In "Bird of Silence," she writes of her mother's rage against her father and his family: "They're no blood relation / to me, my mother once said about my father, / and his side, the Sicilians . . . / She screamed with rage unfamiliar to us both." DeVries concludes the poem, "*To die for,* I say some days, of the memories."

DeVries' passionate language in *How to Sing to a Dago* is sustained throughout her poems. While her images are unique and challenge our usual ways of looking at experience, they never become fanciful or gratuitous flights of the imagination.

This book is an important contribution to Italian American women's poetry.

Where I Come From:
New and Selected Poems
by Maria Mazziotti Gillan

In nearly every poem in *Where I Come From*, Gillan takes a great risk. She has the courage to write about the familiar – family, children, husbands, friends, and mothers. In her free verse form, she makes the common into poetry. She does not strain to create surreal images. Her language is simple and to the point.

Maria Mazziotti Gillan is a teacher of writing and the Director of the Poetry Center at Passaic County Community College in Paterson, New Jersey. She is also the editor of *The Paterson Literary Review* and the author of three previous books of poems. Born in Paterson of southern Italian immigrant parents, Gillan tells us in her poems where she has come from. Behind her strong and assertive yet sensitive voice is an oral tradition that began with anecdotes and stories of her Italian immigrant parents. Other poems are based on her own Italian American experiences as a daughter in her immigrant parents' home and on her experiences as a mother and wife raising a family in Paterson. But whether she is addressing her childhood or her adulthood, the sixty poems in the volume are woven out of a seamless fabric of her Italian American experiences. Gillan has the rare talent to take her domestic and parochial experiences and translate them into moving and profoundly insightful poetry. Her poems tell us as much about our own condition as children, adults, and parents as they inform us about her life.

She recalls in "Public School No. 18 Paterson, N.J." how her teacher humiliated her by demanding that she speak English and by checking her hair for lice in the classroom. Speaking Italian at home, she lived in fear at school that an Italian word would "sprout from my mouth like a rose." In "Eighth Grade," she relates how the teacher went around the room one day dictating who would and would not go to college. When she looked at the olive-skinned, dark-haired Italian girl in the back of the class, she paused, "'You probably will.'" Her teacher's hesitation became "a wound that will never heal / a taste in my mouth cruel and bitter as sin."

In "Talisman" she captures the bicultural conflict of her world. Each morning her mother "pins an evil-eye horn / and scapula to my undershirt." But these amulets did not protect her against her impeccably dressed teacher, Miss Elmer: "Crack! went the ruler across our hands. / Crack! Crack! against small white knuckles." In "Growing up Italian" she contrasts the reality of Italian American life – the language, the food, the family, and neighborhood – with the iconography of American life that she discovered in popular magazines: "I hoped for a miracle that would turn my dark skin light, / that would make me pale and blond and beautiful." Knowing little English when she began grade school, she "grew silent," she writes as "English words fell on me, / thick and sharp as hail." But this is not poetry of victimization. In the end of "Growing Up Italian," she makes it clear she succeeded: "I celebrate / my Italian American self, / . . . Here I am / and I am strong."

She finds an abundance of room in her self for all the parts of her complex life, as daughter, wife, and mother. In a "Love Poem to My Husband," away from home for a week, she writes, "The farther / I move away from you / the more you are with me / . . . Love, / forgive my inattention, / my yearning for a freedom / I do not want." "In Letter to My Mother: Past Due," she reconciles with her mother, asking her, "Come to me in dreams, / knowing I love you / always even when I hurled my rage in your face." As an adult daughter, she can now appreciate her immigrant father's heroic struggle as an unskilled worker, enduring cruel foremen, but in the end surviving with his dignity intact. She was once ashamed of his name,

Arturo, and told her friends when she was young his name was Arthur. At middle age she writes, "Listen, America, / this is my father, Arturo, / and I am his daughter, Maria. / Do not call me Marie."

On a similar theme in "Betrayals" she writes of her father, "How I betrayed you, / over and over, ashamed of your broken tongue." As a mother, with humor and wit she writes that once her son told her, " 'Don't tell anyone you're my mother,' / hunching down in the car / so the other boys won't see us together. Daddy are you laughing? / Oh, how things turn full circle." In "Poem to John: Freshman Year," "My Daughter at Fourteen," and "After the Children Leave Home," she explores the complex emotions of the mother and child relationship. As parents we read these with a sense of recognition of the battles won and lost. Truth rings familiar throughout them all.

These are poems that ultimately transcend their parochial genesis in Gillian's Italian American background. As Diane di Prima writes in her "Afterword," Gillan's poems are "at once a journey home to ourselves, our ancestral customs and beliefs, and outward, to whatever possibilities await us in this ravaged global village. . ." Maria Mazziotti Gillan's poems "illuminate part of the road for us" all.

Gorbachev in Concert (And Other Poems)
by Anne Paolucci

For Anne Paolucci, language is not the enemy of understanding but rather the vehicle for comprehending experience. As she writes in "Poets and Critics": "Even the poet speaks to be over-heard." For Paolucci language does not obfuscate; it illuminates. In "Poetry Festival" she writes: "In due course, meat dressed, / Wine aged, corks checked out for mold, / We'll know if feast / Fit for the gods / Or just editors eating lunch." This is language that leaves a finish on the palate: acidic when she writes with the sharp pen of the satirist and sweet when she addresses the affairs of the heart and soul.

Paolucci's poetry is poetry of place and time. Yet her poems are not merely descriptions of experience. In her hands, language is malleable, like the sculptor's clay. Her respect for the nuances of words and her ability to write in many voices, from the lyrical to the dramatic, makes each page of *Gorbachev in Concert* a surprise and each rereading of her poems a discovery. She exhibits a keen ear for the sharp, hard consonant and the soft long vowel: "Her acolyte in urine-spattered pants" ("Graffiti"); "Broke fast and feasted / On the poet's carcass" ("Chance Meeting"); and "Ribbon trees teach me how to shed my bark" ("Investiture").

While she plays on her words and puns, she extends her metaphors. Her metaphoric webs control her free-verse poems and bind them together: "Like meat aging, / Its own sweet smell of retribution / The quarrel where it grows / Rage is choice game to perfection / Steady in stealth, ravenous revenge, / A feast for one" ("Soliloquy").

But what is, perhaps, most valuable about *Gorbachev in Concert* is that language for Paolucci is not a thing for mere abstract word play. Ultimately, her poems have meaning because they have context. She sees herself as a poet writing within the long history of poetry, Eastern and Western. In "Vying with Petrarch," the lyrical Paolucci asks Petrarch about his Laura, whom he immortalized in his verse: "Who is this woman? / Anyone I know? / And you, poet friend, / Are you still bound to her service / Through chastity to passion? / If she turns to you / Will the poem survive?" These are less questions than they are challenges to the dominant male tradition in love poetry. As an Italian American woman poet, Paolucci had to overcome the silence traditionally imposed upon the common lot of women in Italian culture.

Similarly, in "Dante's 'Pargolette,'" she challenges the idealized image of women in Dante's poems. She brings them all

– "Violets, Matildes, Pietras, Lisettas, Beatices" – down to earth. In her poem young Italian men eye them, "bellybutton nob / Swollen with lust in the exchange / Of greetings beside the Arno." This is love, physical and earthly. In "The Indian in Me," Paolucci declares defiantly, "Let it be known / I slow down for sacred cows / All kinds." In defiance of the image of women in Dante and Petrarch – two of the most important sacred cows in the Western literary canon – she revises the place that women hold in contemporary poetry.

In her historical poems she chooses personages who were visionaries, who slew their own "sacred cows" of tradition. In "Countdown for 1992," Paolucci writes in the voice of an idealistic and even arrogant Columbus who dared challenge tradition: "You ask what I dream? / A map that proves me right, / The heavens chartered, / Another ocean sea to the moon." In "Captain Cook's Vision," a lusty, iconoclastic Captain Cook says, "Down under Blacks with red hair / Recite dusty vaginal tales / The Old West in us all." For a contemporary iconoclast, in the title poem of the volume, "Gorbachev in Concert," she sings a paean to Gorbachev, "the gladiator of an unborn age," who filled the vacuum left by Lenin, who now "guards empty streets / His passion spent."

In "Graffiti," she admires St. Francis and Luther, "opposites" and both iconoclasts. Like them, she considers herself a "congregation of one." She recounts an experience she had with pilgrims she met while visiting Assisi. Her voice barks in the poem, "Screw you / Sweet-smelling hypocrite, / Converted hag, belly-bag of rot." Her lyrical voice can also strike the harsher notes in the vernacular and still make the language sing.

Anne Paolucci's accomplishments are many. She is a poet, fictionist, playwright, and scholar. To her lyrical voice as a poet, she adds her dramatic and narrative styles as both playwright and short story writer. To all her work she brings the scholar's curiosity and intellectual depth. Beginning with her first book of poems in 1977, *Poems Written for Sbek's Mummies, Marie Menken, and Other Important Persons, Places, and Things,* she covers a wide range of subjects in her poems, from ancient myth to the many places she has visited as tourist and visiting scholar. She must be counted among the most important Italian American women poets writing today. In breaking the silence imposed upon her generation of Italian American women, she brings to her work the rich tradition of her particular European past. In her first book she translated Leopardi and wrote poems in Italian, which she translated into English. In *Gorbachev,* her poems on Dante and Petrarch find kinship with Italian Renaissance women poets. Yet in her poems she does not idealize the past, a problem that too often plagues ethnic writing. As she says in "In the Shadow of Darwin": "I took a new world's measure / As far as nature would. I never / Dreamed it would be art."

A Far Rockaway of the Heart
by Lawrence Ferlinghetti

Nearly forty years ago in *Coney Island of the Mind,* Ferlinghetti wrote that the poet constantly takes risks. Each poem is a "death defying leap." In the context of American poetry today that has become nearly moribund with academic, workshop poems, Ferlinghetti's poetry remains as irreverent as it was in the 1950s. His voice is clear and demonstrative. He brings a witty and satiric perspective to his views of art, politics, literature, and middle-class life.

Born in New York, Ferlinghetti traveled to France during World War II where, it is rumored, he became involved in the underground opposing the Nazi occupying forces. He attended the Sorbonne and completed a doctoral degree in literature. He returned to America and settled finally in San Francisco where he established City Lights Books in North Beach. He went on to become a major figure in the Beat Generation.

As an Italian American writer, he was joined in the Beat Movement by Philip Lamantia, Diane di Prima, Gilbert Sorrentino, and Gregory Corso. They were writers who redefined the nature of American writing by bringing it out of the ivy halls of academia and back to common experience in both subject matter and language.

Ferlinghetti's fourteenth book of poems, *A Far Rockaway of the Heart*, is a resurgence of that energetic and irreverent voice that he brought to the Beat Movement in his earlier work. The book contains 101 untitled but numbered poems that embrace the wealth of Ferlinghetti's experiences, from his travels to his experiences with art, music, and literature. In his latest poems, like his earlier work, he turns a critical eye on all aspects of his experiences during his long life. In one poem he depicts a newsboy "announcing the latest lunacy" on the front page of the daily newspaper. He refers disdainfully in another poem to the holocausts of the twentieth century and to "the rape of Cuba and Nicaragua / or Cambodia or Timor," as well as to the shame of the world's ghettos. He centers the blame of this "lunacy" on the narcissism of our age. Ferlinghetti's Narcissus "carried / a small hand mirror / just in case there was no water."

These mirrors are sometimes the museums we build and stock with art that reflect little more than our contemporary absurdity. With disdain he refers to "The party hoppers / wolfing down the wine and cheese" at art openings, comprehending little of what they see. "No wonder," Ferlinghetti writes sardonically, the poor artist "doth drink too much / and roll upon the floor."

In other poems Ferlinghetti waxes enthusiastic over the music of Beethoven, Puccini, Rossini, and Mozart. Their great works create "piercing insights" that lead ultimately "into inner space," the soul of the listener. He writes, too, about the works of Pissarro, Rodin, and Hieronymus Bosch. Pissarro saw an "endless landscape" within his mind, and Rodin was the "realist supreme" and the "Eros eternal." Bosch's monumental painting,

The Garden of Earthly Delights, Ferlinghetti calls a "derisive allegory / of libidinous life on present earth." The lunacy that Bosch saw in the fifteenth century Ferlinghetti sees in the twentieth.

Ferlinghetti turns his wit and satire on the literary lions of this century. He slashes at academic poetry and prose promoted by "gent professors . . . at Columbia." He parodies James Joyce's style, William Carlos Williams' poetic credo, T. S. Eliot's "pathetic phallusies," and Samuel Beckett's "house of cards / made of silence." In a trenchant poem to Ezra Pound, "Confused Confucian / The Rip Van Winkle of American Poetry," Ferlinghetti captures the failure of Pound's tragic career. Pound became an advocate over Rome radio during the war for Mussolini's anti-Semitic fascism. He was arrested in Italy and convicted in the U.S. of treason after World War II. He was incarcerated in St. Elizabeth's mental hospital for eight years as a plea bargain to avoid the death penalty. He lived, until his death in 1972, in a castle in northern Italy in isolation and silence. Even so, Ferlinghetti writes compassionately in the end of the poem of Pound's "enormous dream," the one that lives in his poetry and will outlive his treasonable acts and anti-Semitism. This piece must rank among the best biographical poems ever written.

Ferlinghetti's scope in his collection includes his travels over the last forty years to Paris, Genoa, Rome, Bologna, Florence, and the Greek Islands. Rome for him is "madness and misery / laughter and forgetting." In Bologna, famous for its university sand contentious students, Ferlinghetti writes sardonically that he once joined a "demonstration / against virtual reality / led by Umberto Eco I suppose / or a wit who looks like him."

Where he feels moved, Ferlinghetti can be both lyrical or emotionally expansive. With haiku-like brevity, he writes poems that capture a feeling or an image: the ecstasy of love, a flash of sunlight, a leaf, a hummingbird, or an autumn evening. These he calls "fragile poems" in which "The poet / fathoming the unknown / like a deep ocean trawler / drags for primal images." Elsewhere, Ferlinghetti's measureless poetic voice is in awe of America, from "the iron cities," Ellis Island, Appalachia, the Great Lakes, Amish country, canyons, to the birth places of Thomas Alva Edison and Henry Ford. When impoverished European immigrants came to America, they took refuge in "the wide womb of America."

Much of the success and attraction in Ferlinghetti's poetry is that he knows which notes to play and at what tempo to draw the bow across the strings: *piano, allegro, fortissimo.* When he is moved, he is lyrical. Or when the occasion requires, he is satirical, mocking the foibles of contemporary life. When provoked, he stridently condemns the lunacy that creates poverty, war, and holocausts. No matter where his 101 poems take us – art, literature, travel, politics – they all represent that interior landscape of the poet. He tells us wistfully that he once lived in New York, "But no matter where I wandered / off the chart / I still would love to find again / that lost locality / Where I might catch once more / a Sunday subway for / some Far Rockaway of the heart." Among poets in the post-war period, he is, indeed, *"il miglior fabbro."*

The Moon and the Island
by Laura Stortoni

The Moon and the Island is a book of poems that abounds with the images of women: contemporary, historical, and mythological. As an immigrant and Italian American, Stortoni tells us about the pain of separation – from her native land and family. But the salve for her pain is the balm of remembrance. With it she discovers continuity and affiliation with her past. Her presence in the poems, whether the first person "I" or the dramatic monologue of a mythological goddess, links the poet to all women – past, present, and future. As a result, her separation from Sicily, her homeland, is simultaneously decried and surmounted. We find in each poem a sense of resolve and return. We hear this in the voice of a resolute, independent woman in whatever identity she assumes

A resident of Berkeley, Laura Stortoni was born in Sicily but raised in Milan. She studied abroad and in the U.S. at the University of California, Berkeley. She is a widely published poet and the co-author of two major Italian translations into English: *Gaspara Stampa: Selected Poems* (1994) and *Women Poets of the Italian Renaissance* (1997), both by Italica Press. She has also translated Italian contemporary poets Maria Luisa Spaziani and Giuseppe Conte.

In her Introduction, Diane di Prima writes that "These poems are passionate and sensual, filled with the colors of shells, of red geraniums, the scent of nasturtiums, the sweep of sea and sky, the eyes of children." What distinguishes Stortoni's poems is the hard edge of her imagery. Whether she is capturing an emotion, retelling a Greek myth, or describing the Italian landscape of her Sicilian origins, her poems are built on the bedrock of images. They deliver in quick flashes the poet's memory fragments or the sharp edge of an emotion.

The book's first section, As the Bee Emerges, contains lyrical poems about the self: a young woman who struggles with the bicultural experience in America and confronts life's disappointments, such as the death of her father, divorce, and unrealized hopes. In "A Borrowed Tongue," without her native Italian to serve her in America, Stortoni writes, "Who is poorer than I am? / I can only speak with a borrowed tongue." But in the poems that follow there is a torrent of images and feelings, captured well in an unassuming and unpretentious English.

In "Jealousy," she expresses her feeling of betrayal in the image of an "avocado pit" suspended with tooth picks in a water glass sitting on a windowsill. She imagines that it was placed there by "unknown feminine hands." Her discovery of the budding seed, she writes, "tells me / it's no longer my kitchen." In "Ex-Spouses," the estranged partners are "like / two apprentice acrobats" who have "lost timing." When they meet accidently in "Ex-Spouses Meet at the Local Supermarket," Stortoni captures the moment of sudden embarrassment: "You're fine. I'm fine . . . I wouldntwantyoutothink*Imnot.*" In "The First Thanksgiving after a Divorce," Stortoni writes of the loneliness with no one to speak to or share her meal with: "I will be / my own symposium. . . When the meal is ready / I'll be beautiful – just for myself – / . . . and I'll talk / to the empty chairs." Still, she does not fall victim to self pity. Though she is cheerlessly alone at the table, she concludes with a wry sense of humor and detachment, "But no one listened to me anyway." In "Elegy to My Father," Stortoni pays a belated tribute to her father, especially his love of *The Iliad* and his parsimonious lifestyle. Like all good children, always a day late and an hour short, she regrets her lack of appreciation of him during his lifetime. Stortoni concludes, "Yes, father, I had to bury you to learn how to love you, / you and the things you loved."

Out of these memory shards, Stortoni constructs a strong persona in her poems. In "An Angry Requiem," a poem addressed to a long list of contemporary women writers, Stortoni writes that it would be easy to give up "when Loneliness bites our liver / with its sharp beak." But as she concludes in the title poem of the section, out of the pain and uncertainty of her experiences comes "the possibility of choice." There are possibilities at the end of the twentieth century for women because of the words previous women have written.

In section II, Mediterranean Poems, she writes of those places where she has lived and visited, including Sicily and Milan. In "Sicilian Cities," the cities are "Citadels of memory," of both historical events and personal experiences. In "The Carob Tree," Stortoni recalls a place she once played as a child. In "Breakup in Venice," she merges the historical setting of Venice with her failing marriage, eroding like the decay of the famous

Renaissance city. In "The First Winter after the War," she writes of her family's migration north to Milan. As a Sicilian, she experiences for the first time snow, icicles, and the numbing cold of a northern winter, as well as the deprivations of post-war Italy: "That winter / I learned silence / I learned cold / I learned hunger."

In section III, Personae, the most forceful poems of the volume, Stortoni speaks in the voices of famous women from history and Greek myth. These personae reclaim the voice and the independent image of women that have been overshadowed and nearly lost in Western culture. She begins with a meditation entitled "On Pollaiolo's Portrait of a Renaissance Woman." The image of woman that Stortoni chooses to portray is not that of the conventional Renaissance Madonna but that of a Renaissance painter's image of woman that is aloof, regal, and knowing. In "Artemis," who is the daughter of Zeus and sister of Apollo, the goddess is both a skilled archer and matriarch who defiantly compares her power to her father's. She is an independent goddess who is against monogamy and does not feel bound by the restrictions placed upon women by her clan. As she says of herself, "I am fierce. / I am merciful. / I am undisturbed."

In "Cassandra," the goddess' prophesies are cursed by Apollo and never to be believed. Like nearly all women historically, Cassandra's public voice is discredited. Even so, as a seer, she is burdened with knowledge, even seeing the holocausts of the twentieth century. "But knowledge," she says, "is the hardest thing. / Harder than death." In "Persephone," the Queen of Hades is abducted by Pluto, the god of the underworld. But Persephone is no victim. She tells her mother, Demeter, goddess of agriculture, that she willed her seduction and relishes her independence and solitude in the "chiaroscuro" of her "shadowy kingdom." She says that she looks forward to returning each year, as the goddess of spring, "when I will make the daffodils and the crocus bloom."

In "The Penelope Triptych," Odysseus' wife represents patience, endurance, chastity, and wisdom. Like Cassandra's, her voice, too, is muted by the gods. While Odysseus struggles heroically to return home, she weaves by day and unravels by night. Her artistry is despoiled. Like Cassandra's sagacious soothsaying, Penelope's stability and prudence outweigh her husband's warrior virtues and his epic battle against the will of the gods. She asks, "And who is the hero? The one who departs? The one who stays?" Penelope is the independent artist who is "navigating / the seas of [her] own mind," not the oceans of the known world like her vagrant husband.

In "Anna Comnena Starts to Write the *Alexiad*," the first woman historian, Comnena, writes a history of the exploits of her father, Alexius, in the eleventh century. She is learned and independent. Her book is a record of yet another woman's voice in history. Comnena says that she must speak through her writing. Otherwise, the silence of history will swallow her and her father's exploits. She refuses to unweave by night or be silenced by the gods. She dedicates her history to her subjects: "To them, / and to myself, / I build this monument."

The next two sections of Stortoni's collection contain occasional poems from her variety of experiences. The last section, The Return, brings the reader back to the bicultural experience that is at the center of many of her poems. Here, like her many female personae, her voice assumes mythic dimensions. She is the wanderer, the immigrant, or the fated hero who is caught between two worlds and unable to get home. In "Oranges from the Ancient Orchard," in honor of her grandfather she recalls the orchard where they once walked but which is now a deserted town that she and her relatives had abandoned generations ago. In "How Could They?" she asks "How could my ancestors leave those cities – ?" Because Stortoni cannot entirely explain her own immigration, she shares with her ancestors the pain of separation and the longing to get back. She knows, like most immigrants before her, that she cannot ever truly return. But in "The Return," she exclaims, "Now my song / pierces like a knife: / I am one of the rememberers." Her book of poems becomes her "ziggurat" – her temple of remembrance.

Stortoni is aware of the long history and tradition of women writers in Western culture. As she says in "Angry Requiem," "If the best of us / want only to die . . . who will be left / to carry the pain / on muscular shoulders / for the sisters who are now / in the cradle?" Her poetry is linked to all women writers, from Medieval historian Comnena and Renaissance poet Gaspara Stampa to contemporary women poets, such as Diane di Prima and Maria Mazziotti Gillan. *The Moon and the Island* has earned a deserving place on the shelf with them all.

Sicilian Poetry in America

Malidittu la lingua
by Vincenzo Ancona

Sicilian-born Vincenzo Ancona has been writing poetry in his native language, Sicilian, for more than three decades. As Chairetakis and Sciorra write in their preface, *Malidittu la lingua* (Damned Language) and the audio tapes in the Sicilian accompanying the volume bring together "the two essential elements of Ancona's work, showing that he is indeed a man of two worlds who spans the distance between oral and schooled composition, between the verbal and visual arts, between rural Sicily and urban America."

Vincenzo Ancona was born in 1915 in Castellammare, Sicily. In 1956, with his wife and four children, he immigrated to the United States and settled in Bensonhurst, New York. For the next seventeen years he worked in a broom factory, which he described as "the worst job in the United States." Even so, his life in Bensonhurst became the basis for most of his best poetry.

Sicilian poetry has a long and noble history in Italy. Some of the first poetry written in the vernacular was composed in the Sicilian court of King Frederick II in the thirteenth century. This poetry had a considerable influence on future Italian poets, including Dante. As Luisa Del Giudice writes in her informative introduction, Sicily, long known as the *isola dei poeti*, was home to itinerant bards and street performers who roamed the villages and cities reciting and singing their poetry. Though they sang and wrote in the vernacular, they provided a valuable link between the classical world and modern Sicily. It is this tradition of "spontaneous" Sicilian folk poetry that Ancona brought with him from his native land.

As Del Giudice explains, though Ancona does not write strictly in that "spontaneous tradition," in the topical subject matter of his poetry and in the formal aspects of his meter and rhyme, he represents that bridge in Sicilian poetry that has always existed between folk bards of the street and traditional academic poets. Like his folk predecessors, Ancona's poems focus on common experience. As Giudice explains, classic Sicilian folk poetry often focused on "love, jealousy, separation and scorn." In later years poets began to concentrate on social themes, from poverty to the mafia. Though he makes no pretense of being a street bard, the rhythm of Ancona's lines and his themes still give his poems a refreshing non-academic spontaneity that certainly suggests his roots as a Sicilian folk bard.

To bridge the gap between Ancona's written text and the oral tradition, the bilingual volume is accompanied by a tape of Ancona's reading of his poems. After reading the volume and then listening to the tapes, I discovered that the true essence of Ancona's poems can only be communicated in the original Sicilian. His readings bring each poem on the tape alive with his intonation and rhythm. The tape sadly underscores our loss of the oral tradition in poetry.

The work is divided into several sections: The American Experience, Life in Sicily, Anecdotes, and Tales. The poems, lyrical as well as narrative in form, range in length from six lines to well over a hundred. In "Amerisicula" he writes about the Sicilians in Bensonhurst, "who have turned Brooklyn into their dominion." In others he takes up occasional topics, "Things Happen to Me on a Bus," and "Merry Christmas and I'm Alone." At Christmas mass, a time of joy, he sees a woman crying: *"Si dici bon natali cu è cuntenti, / però pinsamu; soffri tanta genti!"* ("Let those who are happy wish each other joy, / but think of all who suffer on this day!")

In "The Life I Lead," he writes how during an unemployed period in his life he began to make figures and objects fashioned out of wire. The objects, farmers, cowherds, and saints, are all derived from his Sicilian past. During this stressful time, memory is his savior. Ancona concludes, *"Tuttu lu me passatu è na firita, / si ci reflettu; ma chi è sta vita?"* ("It feels then like the burning of a knife, / when I review my past. But what is life?") Memory serves him well in his poems in the section as he writes about incidents, people, and places from his Sicilian past: "A Bandit's Story," "Olive Tree," "The Feast of St. Joseph," and "Portrait of My Town."

In "Damned Language," the title poem of the volume, he speaks of the travails of immigration: *"S'un mi la 'nsignu sugnu ruvinatu, / sta lingua 'nglisi c'un sacciu parrari"* ("If I do not learn English soon, I will be ruined. / Damn this language I don't know how to speak"). In this poem and others, especially "Things Happen to Me Even on a Bus," Ancona writes not just about events typical of the lives of ordinary people, but about the problems that befall those at the bottom of the social ladder. He complains in "Damned Language," *"Pari chi lu distinu lu fa apposta, / Tutti sti cosi succerinu a mia"* (I don't know why! It must be destiny; / these incidents keep happening to me").

Similarly, in the final poem in the volume, "Old Fashioned Father and Modern Son," Ancona has a conversation with his fellow Sicilian American poet, Antonio Provenzano – the Son. Typically, Ancona (the Father) is the butt of most of the humor in the poem and gives the Son all the best lines. In the poem the older Ancona complains about the changes, all of them bad, in the sexual mores of the young. But the ungrateful Son accuses the Father of speaking only out of envy, that he wishes he had had the same freedom in his youth, especially sexual. They go back and forth in the dialogue for pages, and in each round the poor Father is made to appear, with great humor, wildly out of step with contemporary life and today's youth. As the final poem in the volume, "Old-Fashioned and Modern Son," not only expresses the conflict between two generations but the conflict at the basis of Ancona's bicultural experience. It dramatizes the collision between the values of his Old World immigrant experiences and the values of modern society.

Fate always seems to deal Ancona an unworkable hand, something common people to whom his poetry is addressed can understand. But because of his spiritual adaptability, he always manages to survive – a theme that is quintessentially Sicilian. He never becomes a morose victim. Whatever his predicament, he peppers life's unpleasant experiences with his wit and humor. Thus, in his poems he always manages to make a place for himself in the human family.

Vinissi: I'd Love to Come
by Antonino Provenzano

Like Ancona, Anthony Provenzano was born in Castellammare del Golfo, Sicily. After serving his military service in Italy, he immigrated to America and settled in New York, where he currently owns a hair salon in Manhattan and lives with his family on Long Island. He is vice president of Arba Sicula.

Provenzano's interest in poetry began at an early age. As he explains in his introduction, when he was a boy in Castellammare in the early 1950s, villagers would gather around a fire after the grape harvest. While eating the traditional dish of pasta and fava beans, they would recite poetry. In addition, each year Castellammare would host a poetry convention to which poets from around Sicily would come to read and recite their works. He also tells us that in front of the local barber shop or the shoemaker's stall small groups of poets would gather to recite their works nearly every day of his young life. Castellammare was a magnet for the poets of the area. A popular aphorism captures accurately the milieu in which Provenzano grew up: *"cui voli puisia vegna in Sicilia chi porta la bannera di vittoria"*

("If you want to hear poetry come to Sicily. It holds the banner of victory"). He wrote his first poems as an adolescent under the influence of these vernacular street bards. This began a love of poetry in Provenzano's heart that would last a lifetime. But more important, from his earliest experiences he heard poetry recited in idiomatic Sicilian. This was poetry about real people in real-life situations. As Luisa Del Giudice explains in her introduction to Ancona's *Malidittu la lingua*, Provenzano's poems are even closer than Ancona's to that spontaneous Sicilian folk poetry that has its roots in the works of those medieval bards that once roamed the Sicilian countryside.

Prof. Cipolla's English translations of Provenzano's Sicilian capture well his tone and wit. His poems tell the stories of common people and express both the pathos and the humor of their lives. In one, "The Busy Doctor," a poor man with a smashed finger goes to a doctor where he must wait endlessly to be treated. But his fate is better than that of a poor delivery man, mistaken as a patient, who has waited in the office all day: *"E ch'è diri eu chi vinni? / pi purtari un telegramma!"* ("What am I supposed to say? / I just brought a telegram!")

In another humorous poem, Provenzano writes about an Italian office worker who has an easy, secure government job that pays well and does not require much work. The only problem is that his boss snores more loudly than he in the office during the day: *"ma eu 'n supportu li sò runfuluna, / e 'un dormu mancu cu la camumilla"* ("it's just that I can't stand how hard he snores, / and keeps me [awake] because of how he roars").

In another, "Why We Are Italians," with tongue in cheek a father answers his daughter's question about why we are Italians. He explains, *"'Mmagina un munnu senza li spaghetti, / o la lasagna, li ziti 'nfurnati / dda ricca sarsa chi 'ncapu ci metti / ch'è la dilizia di l'umanitati"* ("Imagine then a world without spaghetti, / without lasagne, or without baked ziti, without that savory sauce we put on top, / which is humanity's delight and joy").

As an immigrant, Provenzano also addresses the bicultural theme that is at the center of his consciousness as a poet. In *Vinissi*, he has brought that ancient Sicilian vernacular tradition to America and adds to that tradition the theme of the Sicilian exile. In contrast to his humorous poems, in "There Will Always Be Emigrants," a youthful immigrant laments what he has lost in his resettlement in America. In a similar poem, "Letter to a Politician from a Retired Emigrant," an Italian man complains of the economic injustice done to retired people who have built America. In "Bitter Song to Sicily" (written when Judges Falcone and Borsellino were murdered) Provenzano laments the changes, few for the better, that have come to Sicily: *"Usi e custumi cancianu, / natura cancia puru, / modi viventi e linqua, / mai nenti fermu sta"* (Customs, traditions change. / Nature changes as well, / as do ways, tongues, and men. / Nothing remains the same"). In "The Reed Pipe," the instrument of Sicilian shepherds reminds him of his exile from his country: *"Stasira vogghiu tuttu ricurdari / di la Sicilia e di li so usanzi"* ("Tonight I just want to recall all things, / all the traditions of my Sicily").

There are other vignettes from the lives of scientists, sailors, fathers, and sons, as well as paeans to love, art, peace, brotherhood, and spring. Provenzano is equally at home whether he is writing a narrative or lyrical poem.

Common experience is the wellspring of Provenzano's and Ancona's poetry. Both poets bring into the twentieth century not only the Sicilian oral tradition, but the original source of Western poetry. The revolutions in poetry over the last two centuries, from Wordsworth and Whitman to the Beats in the 1950s, have always sought to return moribund, academic poetry to its original source in both the vernacular and common experience. In that context, Ancona's and Provenzano's poems are a reminder of where poetry not only originated but where it is destined to return if it begins to wander from the hearts and language of common people.

Bibliography

HISTORY, FOLKLORE, AND CRITICISM

Alba, Richard. *Italian Americans: Into the Twilight of Ethnicity*. Englewood Cliffs: Prentice-Hall, 1985.

Balboni, Alan. *Beyond the Mafia: Italian Americans and the Development of Las Vegas*. Reno: University of Nevada Press, 1996.

Barolini, Helen. *Chiaroscuro: Essays of Identity*. West Lafayette: Bordighera, 1997.

Bernardi, Adria. *Houses with Names: The Italian Immigrants of Highwood, Illinois*. Urbana: University of Illinois Press, 1990.

Calvino, Italo, ed. *Italian Folktales*. New York: Harcourt Brace Jovanovich, 1980.

D'Alfonso, Antonio. *In Italics: In Defense of Ethnicity*. Toronto: Guernica, 1996.

Del Giudice, Luisa, ed. *Studies in Italian American Folklore*. Logan: Utah State University, 1993.

Foerster, Robert F. *The Italian Emigration of Our Times*. Cambridge: Harvard University Press, 1919.

Gardaphé, Fred. *Dagoes Read: Tradition and the Italian/American Writer*. Toronto: Guernica, 1996.

——. *Italian Signs, American Streets: The Evolution of the Italian American Narrative*. Durham: Duke University Press, 1996.

Gramsci, Antonio. *Prison Notebooks*. 5 vols. Ed. and Trans. Joseph A. Buttigieg. New York: Columbia University Press, 1996. Vol. 2.

——. *The Modern Prince and Other Writings*. New York: International Pub., 1957.

Gunew, Sneja. "Multicultural Multiplicities: Canada, U.S.A. and Australia." *Social Pluralism and Literary History*. Ed. Francesco Loriggio. Toronto: Guernica, 1996.

Johnson, Colleen L. *Growing Up and Growing Old in Italian-American Families*. New Brunswick: Rutgers University Press, 1985.

LaGumina, Salvatore J. *From Steerage to Suburb: Long Island Italians*. New York: Center for Migration Studies, 1988.

La Sorte, Michael. *La Merica: Images of Italian Greenhorn Experience*. Philadelphia: Temple University Press, 1985.

Loriggio, Francesco, ed. *Social Pluralism and Literary History*. Toronto: Guernica, 1996.

Malpezzi, Frances M. and William M. Clements. *Italian-American Folklore*. Little Rock: August House Publishers, Inc., 1992.

Mangione, Jerre and Ben Morreale. *La Storia: Five Centuries of the Italian American Experience*. New York: HarperCollins Publishers, 1992.

Mathias, Elizabeth and Richard Raspa. *Italian Folktales in America: The Verbal Art of an Immigrant Woman*. Detroit: Wayne State University Press, 1988.

Nelli, Humbert S. *Italians in Chicago: 1880-1930*. Oxford: Oxford University Press, 1970.

Pivato, Joseph. *Echo: Essays on Other Literatures*. Toronto: Guernica, 1994.

Rolle, Andrew F. *The Immigrant Upraised*. Norman: University of Oklahoma Press, 1968.

——. *The Italian Americans: Troubled Roots*. Norman: University of Oklahoma Press, 1980.

Romano, Rose. "Coming out Olive in the Lesbian Community." *Social Pluralism and Literary History*. Ed. Francesco Loriggio. Toronto: Guernica, 1996.

Salvatore, Filippo. *Ancient Memories, Modern Identities*. Toronto: Guernica, 1999.

Sensi-Isolani, Paola A. and Phylis Cancilla Martinelli, ed. *Struggle and Success*. New York: Center for Migration Studies, 1993.

Talese, Gay. "Where are the Italian American Novelists?" *The Columbus People*. Ed. Lydio Tomasi, et. al. New York: Center for Migration Studies, 1994.

Tomasi, Lydio F. , Piero Gastaldo and Thomas Row, ed. *The Columbus People*. New York: Center for Migration Studies, 1994.

Tricarico, Donald. *The Italians of Greenwich Village*. New York: Center for Migration Studies, 1984.

Verdicchio, Pasquale. "Subalterns Abroad: Writing Between Nations and Cultures." *Social Pluralism and Literary History*. Ed. Francesco Loriggio. Toronto: Guernica, 1996.

——. *Devils in Paradise: Writing in Post-Emigrant Culture*. Toronto: Guernica, 1997.

FICTION AND AUTOBIOGRAPHY

Aieta, Vito. *Calabrian Tales*. Cincinnati: Capozzolo Printers, 1989.

——. *From Behind a Chair*. Cincinnati: Capozzolo Printers, 1989.

Barolini, Helen, ed. *The Dream Book*. New York: Schocken Books, 1985.

——. *Umbertina*. New York: Seaview Books, 1979.

Bona, Mary Jo, ed. *The Voices We Carry*. Toronto: Guernica, 1994.

Carilli, Theresa. *Women as Lovers*. Toronto: Guernica, 1996.

D'Alfonso, Antonio. *Fabrizio's Passion*. Toronto: Guernica, 1995; 2nd edition, 2000.

De Luca Calce, Fiorella. *Vinnie and Me*. Toronto: Guernica, 1996.

De Rosa, Tina. *Paper Fish*. New York: The Feminist Press, 1996.

Di Donato, Pietro. *Christ in Concrete*. New York: Penguin Books, 1993.

Edwards, Caterina. *The Lion's Mouth*. Toronto: Guernica, 1993; (original: 1982).

Mangione, Jerre. *Reunion in Sicily*. New York: Columbia University Press, 1984.

Micone, Marco. *Beyond the Ruins*. Toronto: Guernica, 1995.

Mirabelli, Eugene. *The World at Noon*. Toronto: Guernica, 1994.

Pellegrini, Angelo. *American Dream*. San Francisco: North Point Press, 1986.

Rimanelli, Giose. *Benedetta in Guysterland*. Toronto: Guernica, 1993.

Tucci, Niccolò. *The Rain Came Last and Other Stories*. New York: New Directions, 1990.

Viscusi, Robert. *Astoria*. Toronto: Guernica, 1995.

Vivante, Arturo. *Run to the Waterfall*. New York: Charles Scribner's Sons, 1979.

POETRY

Ancona, Vincenzo. *Malidittu la lingua*. New York: Legas, 1990.

DeVries, Rachel Guido. *How to Sing to a Dago*. Toronto: Guernica, 1996.

Ferlinghetti, Lawrence. *A Far Rockaway of the Heart*. New York: New Directions, 1997.

Maviglia, Joseph. *A God Hangs Upside Down*. Toronto: Guernica, 1994.

Mazziotti Gillan, Maria. *Where I Come From*. Toronto: Guernica, 1995.

Paolucci, Anne. *Gorbachev in Concert*. New York: Griffon House Publications, 1991.

Provenzano, Antonino. *Vinissi: I'd Love to Come*. New York: Legas, 1995.

Raptosh, Diane. *Just West of Now*. Toronto: Guernica, 1992.

Stortoni, Laura. *The Moon and the Island*. Berkeley: Hesperia Press, 1997.